AF565102

The Room of Delight

The Room of Delight

Oldrich Otypka

SOUTH BRUNSWICK AND NEW YORK: A. S. BARNES AND COMPANY
LONDON: THOMAS YOSELOFF LTD

A. S. Barnes and Co. Inc.
Cranbury, New Jersey 08512

Thomas Yoseloff Ltd
108 New Bond Street
London W1Y OQX, England

Library of Congress Cataloging in Publication Data

Otypka, Oldrich 1921-
The room of delight.

Bibliography: p.
Includes index.
1. House plants. 2. Garden rooms. I. Title.
SB419.084 1974 635.9'82 73-22598
ISBN 0-498-01467-3

PRINTED IN THE UNITED STATES OF AMERICA

To my wife and children,
who enjoy our
Room of Delight
with me

Contents

Acknowledgments

A book about plants is a collection of knowledge and experience, to which a person arrives through his own efforts and with the help of others. I would like to express my thanks to:

Commercial growers who allowed me to roam through their greenhouses and willingly discussed the problems of raising plants.

Many of my friends for sharing the knowledge and experience of growing flowers and the discussions in which many ideas were clarified and enriched.

Mr. Rudolph Ziesenhenne, the Nomenclature Director of The American Begonia Society, for information about some begonias, which I was unable to obtain elsewhere.

My daughter Marcella for proofreading of the manuscript and correcting my English "frazes."

To all mentioned above, my grateful: Thank you!

Introduction

An indoor garden—the Room of Delight—can be called the room of the future: part of the house set aside, not only for plants, but for people's relaxation. In the healthful, oxygen-filled atmosphere created by plants, it is pleasure to sit, rest, talk, eat—or simply observe blossoms to the music of bubbling and splashing water. Such a room is made for plants by people and for people by plants. Without flowers, the garden room would not have its charm and restful atmosphere. Without human effort and attention, the plants would not survive. This mutual dependence brings mutual appreciation and satisfaction, a true cooperation resulting in an indoor garden that everyone will like and admire.

The Room of Delight

1
The Room of Delight

In my teens I visited a famous castle in my native Czechoslovakia. One feature of that castle made a permanent impression on me. Not that a castle was something new. As a student, I spent the summer vacations with my uncle, where I literally lived in the shadows of huge castle buildings. Almost every day I wandered in extensive parks surrounding the castle. I never tired of its flower beds, intriguing walks, statues surrounded with special-effect planting, the huge seashell on a pedestal standing in the circle of tall pines, almost undiscernable transition of parks into forests, the beautiful vistas of two valleys, the Lower Park way below, and the city in the distance, sitting on the plains.

The visit to the castle of Lednice was a routine classroom excursion and I was greatly impressed with that famous palace. The rooms were unusual, richly furnished, ceilings covered with intricate carvings executed in exotic woods. The beautiful park was enormous, with lakes, vistas, and a number of garden temples scattered around.

Yet what made the greatest impression on me was a conservatory attached to one wing of the castle. Its vaulted glass roof looked rather strange next to the neo-gothic architecture of the palace. However, its utility was evident. Only a few steps were necessary from a dark corridor—and you entered into daylight brightness of the conservatory. Through the center a small brook was bubbling over a pebbled bed. In two places the brook was enlarged into ponds stocked with goldfish. Walks of compacted gravel led throughout, to an elevated section and along smartly designed plantings. A number of benches were inviting to sit amidst this wonder. What a surprise! I never saw anything like that before: the beauty of a year-round garden only few steps from living quarters.

In the following years my mind turned many times to that conservatory, especially during the confinement of winter months. Slowly the vision of the home conservatory developed into a dream.

It took many years before the dream could be converted into reality. When finally the time came of planning and building, it as a time filled with anticipation: how enjoyable that room would be! And the fulfillment even surpassed all my expectations.

My little conservatory did not come easily. In order to have it I had to perform many tasks myself. All concrete work and drainage for plumbing was done by the contractor. The superstructure, the assembly of heavy beams and Plexiglas roof, was my task. With the help of my wife, I hoisted the beams and roof panels into place. It was laborious. With the installation of large windows, my wife also helped.

When I was finally done with the heating system just before the cold weather arrived, we found there is much to be learned about the plants and special conditions of our delightful room.

As typical Northerners we wanted to have miniature orange and lemon trees—a proof that since the first orangery was built the citrus tree did not lose its magic attraction for the people of severe winter climates. The rose trees were next on the

Author's Room of Delight.

list of desired plants. Cannas were planted next to the glass wall. The coffee tree was not omitted either, for its curiosity and glossy green leaves. Everblooming Impatiens were put next to the Cannas, where they are protected by the barrier of heating installation from direct sun.

We use our delightful room year around, not only to sit, read, and study, but also to eat and to entertain friends. The room, full of light, sunshine, fragrance, and sounds of splashing water, is attractive day after day. The appearance of plants changes constantly according to the available light. The bright sunshine allows the display of all different shades of greenery and colors of blossoms to their best advantage. And when days get shorter and the low sun is getting ready to set, our indoor garden is filled with streams in red, orange, or gold.

Not even at night does that delightful room lose attraction. On nights when the moon reigns over the sky, its light covers everything with a mantle of silver: the orange trees glitter, large leaves of *Begonia ricinifolia* shine in satin green, and the splashing drops of water are like drops of mercury. You gaze at that beauty, gaze at the moon that causes such a panorama, and you are unwilling to exchange the silver carpet for your bed.

The harmony of colors, forms, or simply the presence of living plants create an indoor garden of unusual atmosphere. Only sheets of glass separate this flowering beauty from the killing frost in winter or the devastating forces of wind in summer. Such a protective environment is beneficial to the plants and equally enjoyed by people. The pleasant warmth and humidity, the beauty and company of living plants make our indoor garden very inviting and attractive: a perpetual garden, only a few steps from living areas, to be enjoyed every day of the year—truly, a room of delight.

The boyhood dream is fulfilled: I have a conservatory. It is not attached to a castle and is not extra large—rather small, yet very lovely.

2

The Garden Necessity

Gardens, as we know them, are areas of delight. Normally we do not consider as such the gardens for raising vegetables or herbs for culinary or medicinal purposes.

The gardens surrounding a house or a villa have the greatest impact. Although people always liked plants next to their places of living, it was not always possible to enjoy them in such a manner. Gardens are a fragile establishment requiring space, freedom for maintenance, and security from destruction. These requirements were not always available, security being the chief problem. Marauding armies of soldiers and bandits compelled people to live in fortified cities and castles, where there was not enough space for nature. Tiny gardens in the city and a few raised beds for herbs and flowers in a fortified castle were a luxury.

Such a situation was tolerated only under the pressure of insecurity and danger of attack. The greatest security known to the ancient world arrived a few decades before Christ. Bringing the civil wars to an end, Augustus brought peace and prosperity to the Roman Empire. To safeguard peace, the dangerous boundaries were fortified and guarded by well-disciplined and equipped legions. About that time people grew tired of their city culture and desired nature, life in the countryside. Such desire found its best expression in bucolics, pastoral poems glorifying nature and the life of carefree shepherds. The author was Virgil, the greatest Roman poet. Son of a farmer, he introduced nature in an idealized form to the city people and thus ushered in the great rush into the open country. Beautiful villas were built, sitting in the middle of pleasure gardens. The best architects, artists, and gardeners were called on to create well-landscaped areas.

The gardens were not simply areas of countryside. Skillfully planted trees, bushes, and flower beds were enlivened with statues in marble and bronze, interlaced with walks and benches and cooled by fountains and brooks. Villas and beautiful gardens were built not only in the vicinity of Rome and other cities. Virgil himself and other rich citizens built villas as far as the shores of lakes in northern Italy, where the majestic Alps provide cooler and more comfortable summers.

For more than four hundred years that happy association of people with nature lasted. In the fifth century A.D. the onslaught of barbaric nations broke the bulwark of frontier fortifications and sent the demoralized legions into flight. In a relatively short time, the culture of the West Roman empire disappeared and with it the villas and gardens. People again sought refuge in fortified cities and castles, where they were generally separated from nature except on short excursions into the countryside.

The idea of living in villas surrounded by gardens was brought again to light in the fifteenth century by humanists and their studies of antiquity. The humanists not only studied the ancient Greco-Roman world; they eagerly tried to imitate it. Some were obsessed with the culture of the ancient world. Jan ze Stredy, chancellor to Emperor Charles IV and later the bishop of Olomouc, Czechoslovakia, invoked the blessings of Greek and Roman gods in almost every letter he wrote. It was a strange act of a bishop, who daily recited the prayers of the Church from his breviary, beautifully adorned with miniature paintings of Jesus Christ and His saints. Some seventy years later Ciriaco d'Ancona, a Florentine traveler and discoverer of many buried treasures of classical art, used to pray for safe journey to his "most holy patron, fleet-footed Mercury,"* the Roman god of travelers.

The city of Florence in Italy was the focal point of the revival of classical studies and arts. When descriptions of Roman villas and gardens were discovered in the old manuscripts, the Florentines started to build them, being faithful to the classical example. Florence's leading family, Medici, was the first one to build several villas and gardens adorned with statues and fountains. Few followed their example. History almost repeated itself. In ancient Rome the great boom of building villas and gardens in the first century B.C. was also preceded by some excellent villas, the best of them being built by the famous millionaire Lucullus. However, people were reluctant to abandon the fortifications. The first villa, built about 1487 in Rome, was located within the defense walls of the Vatican. Villas Madama and La Farnesina with their beautiful gardens, built thirty years later outside the walls of Rome, were built for entertainment only and not to be lived in.

The large-scale acceptance of gardens and villas was not brought on by further studies of examples of ancient Rome. If the Romans started to build their villas and gardens when the era of civil wars ended and peace and security set in, the boom in building villas and gardens in the sixteenth century was triggered by just the opposite. The cause was shattered security, crumbling under the bombardment of cannons. The reason that villas were first built near the capitals of Italian city republics was the security afforded by the defenses of the cities. Such security did not exist for everybody, however. Therefore, the aristocracy continued to build fortified castles, until the effective bombing of improved artillery convinced them of the futility to hide behind the thick walls.

That realization was a slow process growing out of the bitter experiences the Italians went through in the first thirty years of the sixteenth century. Up to that time Italy was the richest country in Europe and, as such, a coveted prize of conquest. France opened the campaign for domination of Italy. Soon Germany and Spain were drawn into the conflict, converting all of northern Italy into a vast battleground. The invaders brought not only better and more efficient artillery, but also a new type of bloody warfare.

The wars that Italian republics and principalities used to have among themselves were a kind of costly game: slow, long, and "battles commonly ended with few or no casualties"—as romantically comments the diplomat and historian Giucciardini. However, to the invaders, war was not a game, but a bloody affair in which the attaining of military objectives was superior to casualties, losses among civilians and works of art. For such a kind of warfare, the invaders earned the title *barbarians*.

The impact of those wars on Italy was enormous. Few fortified cities and castles could withstand the siege of the cannons. "The French artillery could do as much damage in few hours, what to the Italian [oxen drawn] artillery used to take days," remarked historian Giucciardini, himself a military commander. The lesson was not drawn immediately, and what is more interesting, not in devastated northern Italy. It took another fifteen years and a distance of three hundred miles from the major battlefields to realize that inaccessible location and thick walls could not any longer protect from the bombardment of the cannons.

How thinking was changing can be seen in the castle of the family Farnese. At the height of the wars for the domination of Italy, in 1525, the Farnese family started to build a fortified castle on a hill behind the village Caprarola, thirty-five miles north of Rome. In 1547 Cardinal Alessandro Farnese commissioned the famous architect Vignola to rebuild the fortress into a pleasure castle. That far-reaching decision must have been crystallizing for a long time, because the great Cardinal had, for thirteen years already, owned the well-known villa La Farnesina outside the walls of Rome, which, however, was built for entertainment only. Vignola rebuilt the Caprarola into a pleasure castle, incorporating in the design the deep moat and corner bastions. The palace, built on the mas-

*Vincent Cronin. *The Florentine Renaissance*. Published by E.P. Dutton & Co., Inc. and used with their permission.

sive base of the former fortifications, appears like a triumph of beauty over false security. And the beautiful garden behind only reaffirms that victory.

Caprarola, built so far away from a city, was the first one to abandon fortifications. Its example was followed a few years later by many palaces and villas surrounded by beautiful gardens. Virtually every outstanding villa and garden in Italy is dated after the year 1547.

The rest of Europe was not convinced. Many kings and noblemen admired the achievements of the Italians and called Italian architects to design garden structures for them. But these were mostly summer pavilions, located within the city or just outside. Basically the fortifications were not abandoned. It took the Thirty Year War, which ended in 1648, and all its destruction, to show that fortifications cannot assure security from the bombardment of improved artillery.

Again, as before in Italy, the awakening to this fact did not come in Central Europe, which bore the brunt of the war. This time, recognizing the change, was the distant France. The French followed the example of Italian villas and gardens, but executed with grandeur and on a large scale. It was in the year 1661 that the great landscape architect Le Notre finished the first open-type gardens around the new palace in Vaux-le-Vicomte, which served as a prototype of Versailles's immense complex of pleasure castles and gardens.

The example of France was eagerly followed by the rest of Europe. The fashion was to abandon the fortified castle, rebuild it or to erect a new palace with a large garden on another location. Noblemen did it without much hesitation. They had reason for it. The fortresses were like jails to their occupants, and even when built in the countryside, sat as if in the middle of a desert. Old engravings show all slopes from defense walls down, barren and void of all vegetation. Trees and bushes would obstruct the visibility of defenders and provide hideout and protection to the enemy. Only much later, these slopes were forested or converted into parks.

Although Europe generally accepted villas and pleasure gardens in the seventeenth century, an attempt to introduce this better side of life was made much earlier. The island of Sicily was conquered in the ninth century by Saracens who soon constructed, near Palermo, a series of parks with Moorish garden structures. Later rulers of Sicily, the Norman and German kings, liked the idea of villas and gardens and tried to introduce them to Southern Italy, which they also ruled. But without success. The Saracen emirs brought the villas and gardens from another area—the security of the Arab world. The Mohammedans enjoyed great external security behind the shield of their armies, on a steady march after more territories. Italy and Europe, however, did not enjoy such security, and therefore did not accept in the twelfth and thirteenth centuries villas and gardens in open countryside—the product of security of a different world.

It is hard to imagine that in the Roman Empire people enjoyed almost absolute security for such a long time. For more than four hundred years, most lands did not see a foreign army and did not experience war on their soil. For about the same length of time, people have been enjoying the revival of the Roman villas and gardens, that are now built, not under absolute security, but under a frustrated security. Our external security exists only in the presence of constant threat of destruction.

It is more remarkable that people were, and are, able to enjoy not only life in the open countryside, but also to build, maintain, and enjoy the gardens of an artificial climate, which are even more subjected to neglect and destruction.

3

Artificial-climate Gardens

The great gardens were developed in the area of the Mediterranean Sea, where climate is subtropical, winters short and mild, consisting of the welcomed rainy season. The gardens were actually enjoyed year round.

When in sixteenth century the power and wealth slowly started to shift to the north of the Alps, to central and northern Europe, the design of gardens accompanied the march of wealth. However, there was one slight disadvantage over the gardens of Italy: the use of the gardens was limited to the short summers. Winters in central and northern Europe are long and cold.

The desire for enjoyment of plants during the winter months gave the start to the enclosed gardens. The beginnings were simple, but with the progress of technology the covered gardens evolved into better and larger climatic wonders. The culmination in building of conservatories came in Europe around the beginning of the twentieth century. Some fifty years later the trend resumed in the United States, with yet larger and better enclosures for tropical plants and the relaxation of people.

The enjoyment of tropical atmosphere provided by unusual plants is the driving force behind the artificial climate gardens. It can be safely said that it all started with the orange. In the sixteenth century, Renaissance Italy became the destination of travelers from the North, tired of centuries-old gothic culture. Italy developed a new style of architecture, sculpture, and painting. The economy was at its height, sufficient money was on hand to keep architects and artists busy. Fortunately, there was an abundance of talented people who provided an uninterrupted stream of works of art. Even if it sounds incredible, the Renaissance reached its peak during the series of foreign invasions. Perhaps, because of those invasions, the new Italian art became better known to the other nations. Europe was astonished. Whoever had money and was able to travel across the Alps rushed to sunny Italy to see the new wonders. But Italy had something else to offer besides paintings, statues, and beautiful villas sitting in magnificent gardens. Just as the appearence of Renaissance art was new—so was the orange, which only in the beginning of the sixteenth century arrived from India to Portugal. In the mild climate of Italy the orange thrived and spread, to the enjoyment of local people and the fascination of travelers from the North. The fragrance of the flowering orange and its delicious fruit were unknown in the North. Nobody could carry away the wall of a building enchanted with paintings and statues or formed in marble. But the seedlings and seeds of the orange were easily transported. That was the beginning of the movement of subtropical plants into the hostile northern climate.

At first it was attempted to grow oranges in the houses, or better in the mansions and castles, of noblemen. Quite soon it was realized that the new arrivals from sunny Italy needed more light than was available in the dwellings. Summers were spent outside; for winter they were moved into special structures with large windows, something we would call a covered porch. It was a forerunner of our conservatory. A new name was coined for such structures: *orangery*. After the Thirty Year War the orange became a craze in Europe and the orangery a status sumbol. The largest orangery, which is 1258 feet long and 45 feet high, was built at Versailles, France, to house in winter 1200 orange trees and over 400 other tropical plants.

The orange held Europe in a spell until the middle of the eighteenth century. By that time, frequent shipments of new exotic plants were arriving in Europe and the domination of the orange was at an end. Orangeries with solid roofs were slowly replaced by greenhouses to house the exotics from North and South America, Africa, Asia, and Australia. And the plants were not arriving singly. In 1759, when the range of greenhouses attached to the imperial palace was finished in Vienna, Austria, it was filled with six shiploads of plants from the Caribbean and South America. Indeed, there was a tremendous quantity needed to fill greenhouses stretching for a length of 1,250 feet.

The nineteenth century brought better heating. Steam and hot water systems were developed to heat large enclosures. As the century progressed, so did the gardens of artificial climate. Greenhouses changed into conservatories, which served not only for the accumulation and wintering of exotic plants, but primarily for the enjoyment of their owners. Pools were carefully masked with greenery; winding paths led from low bushes to towering palms and to the mass of flowering plants. Benches at pools or beneath tropical trees were inviting to rest and to contemplate the unusual beauty.

Most effective and useful were conservatories attached to the living quarters, which became another great room for entertainment and doubled as a sitting room. Besides the personal use of their owners, conservatories were also show rooms of unique exotic plants, often purchased at great expense.

The importance and impact of artificial-climate gardens on botany and plant discoveries are seldom considered. Without indoor gardens it would take much longer to discover many tropical plants. The indoor gardens were in great need of exotics. This demand opened new worlds to the people. New professions were established. Professional plant hunters were unknown before. But the demand for tropicalia sent men on adventurous and dangerous journeys into the unknown interiors of Africa, the Americas, Asia, and Australia. The plant hunters collected unusual and spectacular plants, which were shipped to the specialized nurseries in Europe. Shipments of exotic plants were frequent, numerous, and often large. One of the most successful plant hunters, Benedict Roezl, a native of Czechoslovakia, once sent eight tons of orchids in a single shipment from the jungles of South America. Many unusual plants were sold at auctions in London, England, for fantastic prices. In the second half of the nineteenth century, some orchids were sold for three hundred, five hundred, or one thousand British pounds per single plant. That would be $1,350, $2,250, or $4,500 at a time when wages of skilled workers in the United States were $250-300 a year; in Europe a skilled worker was paid even less. Not only orchids commanded such high prices; the first Rex *Begonias* were selling for $1,930 a piece at the same time.

In the late nineteenth century the demand for tropical plants was insatiable as conservatories grew larger and more numerous. This trend abruptly ended in World War I, with its destruction, scarcity of fuels, and general impoverishment of the nations. Nobility lost its power, prestige, and wealth, which started to shift slowly to the masses of people. Education and luxuries of life—as well as conservatories—were no longer the privileges of the few.

After World War II, a new trend appeared in artificial climate gardens. Small greenhouses started to spring up next to houses in cities, suburbs, and the countryside. Mass production, use of permanent materials like aluminum and plastics, and simple and cheap heating systems, put ownership of a greenhouse within the reach of the middle class. Today more people enjoy tropical plants in their home greenhouses than at the height of the conservatory era in the nineteenth century. In Great Britain, at that time, were several thousands of indoor gardens. Now in that country are more than two million small, private greenhouses.

The mass production of greenhouses is accompanied by mass production of plants. Since greater numbers of people are enjoying tropical plants and buying them, the price of unusual exotics is very low. In 1858, the first Rex *Begonias* cost the equivalent of six or seven years of a worker's wages. Today, a similar *Begonia,* even in better colors, sells for two or three dollars; it can be easily purchased with one hour of work. The orchids are more expensive. But even the price of seven dollers for the cheapest *Dendrobium* in flowering size or a beautiful *Vanda*, branched and with buds, for seventy-five dollars is not much, when compared with the orchids auctioned at fantastic prices in the nineteenth century.

The indoor garden is an easy reality, not only a greenhouse—better yet a room full of plants where to sit is pleasure, to eat is more enjoyable, and where conversation is relaxation: the garden room, the room of delight.

4

The Garden Room

The frequent appearance of a home conservatory (garden room) is hindered by two misunderstandings. The first one represents the home conservatory as a display room for flowers that are raised in separate greenhouses. Such a description is found in almost every book. The second misunderstanding is propounded by the concept of greenhouse gardening. Wherever the hobby greenhouse and its activities are mentioned, greenhouse gardening is an indispensable part of it. For every month of the year is suggested which plants to start, raise, and how to prepare for the next month's task.

Any mentioning of both ideas discourages many people from having a garden room. The first misunderstanding comes from the times when home conservatories were an exclusive hobby of the very rich. Gardeners took care of such conservatories and their supporting greenhouse ranges. That era is gone, and home conservatories can be the property of not so rich people, who are raising plants for their own pleasure without paid gardeners.

The misunderstanding of greenhouse gardening comes from copying commercial greenhouses. Not only are books published, telling how to make a profit from a hobby greenhouse, but home greenhouses are presented as a replica of commercial greenhouse activity.

However, anybody can enjoy plants in a home conservatory without greenhouse gardening and without an additional space where plants are raised for showing off in the garden room. The solution is proper selection of plants. A number of plants are everblooming. Some of them, like *Impatiens* and *Browallia*, should be treated as annuals for the best results. Most of the others will increase production of blooms with age and size. Many other plants bloom several times a year without any maintenance. Large numbers of plants supply beautiful, colorful, or variegated foliage all year and interesting flowers also. The elimination of plants that go dormant, or using only a few, will greatly reduce the work and extra care.

All the beauty of flowers and foliage can be enjoyed with a minimum of maintenance, consisting of weekly clean-up, occasional repotting, and desired propagation for increasing the numbers. The only requirements are sufficient light, proper watering, proper temperature and humidity. The ultimate is to surround oneself with insect-free plants, to eliminate insect problems and the necessary spraying.

Since all the plants in a garden room are tropicals, the night temperature should not be lower then 60° F. Daylight temperatures of 70° F and more are necessary for good growth and flowering. High humidity is as important as temperature and should be maintained in the range of fifty to sixty percent and even higher. Some plants, like *Columneas,* do not bloom much at lower humidity.

Sufficient light is most important for proper growth. For that reason, conservatories are glass enclosures. Few of the plants in a conservatory require direct sunlight. *Citrus, Bougainvilleas, Cannas*, Chinese hibiscus, and succulents are some. The great majority of tropical plants want filtered light in various degrees, much as in their natural habitat, where the thick canopy of trees protects them from direct sunlight.

A good number of tropical plants have the ability to adapt to very low light levels and some also to very low humidity levels. Such plants make it possible to have a nice garden room without the glass roof, something like an enclosed porch, where windows — possibly aided by skylights — are the only sources of light.

Regardless of the enclosure, the garden room differs from a greenhouse. The absence of greenhouse benches makes the entire floor space available for the movement of people and plants. The garden room is primarily a place of relaxation as much as the greenhouse is a place of work. Besides the plants, which enliven the garden room, a certain amount of space is taken up by tables, chairs, and comfortable seats. A water fountain, no matter how small, should be included and given a prominent spot. The bubbling and splashing water is a great source of relaxation and provides a gardenlike atmosphere.

Plants and water constitute the natural elements of a home conservatory. Without them we would have just another room of the house. The location of these elements should be considered carefully. The fountain and the plants are stars of the show in the room of delight. People are spectators. The water fountain, expecially if fitted with statuary, tries to attract attention by forms and sounds; plants compete with a display of blossoms and foliage.

Plants should be located to their best advantage. In the beginning the majority of them will most probably be small. All plants have a different rate of growth, but smaller plants should be located closer to the source of light than taller ones. If it is vice versa, the taller plants rob the smaller of the necessary light, unless light comes from all directions, as in an all-glass enclosure.

When possible, ground beds twelve to sixteen inches deep should be included in the design. Some plants love the freedom afforded by ground beds and do best there. Orange and coffee trees, *Cannas*, palms, passion flower, or any vigorous climber, like ground beds. Other plants like *Chrysanthemums, Geraniums*, and some *Begonias* must be restricted by the confines of a flower pot, if we want abundant production of blossoms. Where ground beds are located along the outside wall, insulation should be provided between the wall and soil. Building quality Styrofoam, one or one-and-half-inch thick, is easily glued on the foundation wall and gives an excellent protection from freezing and low temperatures of soil in the ground beds.

If ground beds are of concrete they must be sealed with epoxy paint. Concrete itself is alkaline and when left exposed the roots of any plant will start to leach the lime from the concrete. Few plants in an indoor garden need alkaline soil. The great majority need neutral or slightly acid soil. Althought many plants are alkali-tolerant, others might rebel and show it with yellowing of the leaves.

The ground beds give rise to another question: What kind of floor in the garden room? One of two approaches can be followed: naturalistic or formal.

The naturalistic approach tries to make the garden room look like an actual garden: all floor is soil, walks are of compacted gravel, flagstone, or other paving material. The majority of plants are planted directly in the ground, and potted ones are sunken up to the rim in the soil.This solution is very effective and probably the best. Large areas of soil keep the humidity high. However, it has its drawbacks. The movement of plants, people, and furniture is restricted, and soil, even mud, is carried into the house proper.

The formal approach is to treat the garden room like any other room of the house: the floor, except ground beds, is solid, covered with desired floor covering. The most practical and inexpensive material is indoor-outdoor carpet. The formal approach affords greater mobility of people, plants, and furniture. Dirt is not carried into the house and floor is easily cleaned, especially when carpet is used. Vacuum cleaning is easy and fast. The only disadvantage of such a floor is the absence of moisture—holding soil, and a humidifier is a necessity.

The separation of the garden room from the house is mandatory. Plants differ from people in their requirements of temperature, humidity, and ventilation. The night temperature of 60° F is necessary for blooming of many winter plants like *Chrysanthemums, Poinsettias,* Christmas cactus, and *Begonias*. The remainder of plants like it cooler at night also, although few people would prefer to sleep at 60° F. Higher humidity is very important for tropical plants. It is more difficult to maintain the whole house at a higher humidity level than to supply enough moisture to just one room. Also the separation of the garden room is necessary when spraying for insects and for summer ventilation, which is necessary for reducing the heat build-up due to large glass areas.

The barrier between the house and garden room should not be solid. It is best to make the garden room visually part of the house by installing large windows, a glass wall, or glass sliding doors. In this way, all the beauty of the plants can be enjoyed also from the house.

When we are talking about a garden room or home conservatory, we have in mind a room that is warm, with lowest night temperature of 60° F. In such a room will grow a wide variety of tropical plants but will be excluded others needing cooler night temperatures. Anyone wanting to grow and bring to bloom *Geraniums, Camellias, Cyclamen, Freezias, Hyacinth*—to name only few—will have to keep his garden room temperatures at night at 45° - 50° F and during the day at 60° - 65° F. But in that case it would be necessary to take into account the lower temperatures and supply the room adjacent to the conservatory with more heat.

It is not advisable to try to mix cold and warmth loving plants in one room and expect good results. The decision must be made in design stages. If you want a garden room, the room of delight, it has to be kept warm for plants and people. The exclusion of cold-loving plants is mandatory with the exception of few *Azaleas* and *Geraniums*, which can be grown in some cold corner.

5

The Room with Light-transmitting Roof

The garden room is an indoor garden with the transparent enclosure to provide maximum available light. Glass enclosures for plants have been made for more than two hundred years. First used for greenhouses, later adapted for magnificent domes and huge structures of conservatories, the glass enclosure is the best type for a garden room. Recently the glass for large domes or small greenhouses has been displaced by plastic materials like Plexiglas or fiberglass, which have the advantage of unbreakability and possibility of greater spans.

Any garden room can have the same enclosure as a greenhouse, which is available from many sources. Greenhouse structures come in many different shapes, not only rectangular, but also circular. In the rectangular shape two basic types are recognized: *the even span* and *lean-to structure*. The even span has a roof ridge at the high point and from it the roof slopes on two sides. This type provides the maximum light availability, since the light comes from all sides. The lean-to does as its name says: it leans to the house. The roof is attached at its highest point to the wall of an existing structure. The lean-to is much cheaper, and although it does not provide the maximum light, it is sufficient and very economical.

Today's greenhouses are made of very durable materials. Aluminum and redwood are used almost exclusively. Aluminum is rust-proof and does not need any maintenance—yet it has its drawbacks, too: condensation of moisture forms easily and, for an indoor room, it has a little cold and foreign effect. Redwood is more acceptable for the garden room, since it has a soft and pleasing appearance. However, when redwood weathers, its look is appalling to many people. This can be easily overcome by staining either new or weathered wood. Creosote-treated wood cannot be used in an indoor garden. Creosote fumes, released from treated wood, will kill plants.

Greenhouse structures are easily available. Every gardening magazine carries a number of advertisements. Many firms offer the catalogs free. All greenhouse structures are shipped precut, with all necessary glass, door, windows, and other accessories. Any handyman, with some help, can erect such a house, or it can be assembled by a professional carpenter or metal worker.

It should be noted that a garden room must be built on a proper foundation, going below the frost line. This is usually thirty-six to forty-two inches or less, depending on locality. The necessity of a foundation is not the weight of the structure, but the heaving action of the frost. If any moisture is present in the soil under the foundation and it freezes, the soil acts like a swollen texture. Since it can expand only upwards, which is the direction of the least resistance, it lifts whatever is on top of it. Movements of several inches are sometimes encountered. If such a movement is applied to a greenhouse structure, glass breaks, wood cracks, and metal is twisted. It is necessary to find out what is the minimal depth of foundations in the locality in question and then direct the construction of footings accordingly.

Since the garden room is a special-effect room, to be used primarily for relaxation, the glazing should be considered more carefully than glazing of a greenhouse, which is exclusively a working area. Greenhouses are generally provided with a single sheet of glass. When the outside temperature drops below freezing, the high moisture content in the air starts to condense on the inside of the glass panes. If the outdoor temperature is very cold, the glass itself is below freezing point. Then the moisture that is condensed on the glass freezes and forms the familiar "Jack Frost" paintings. These "paintings" do not occur if the sun is shining on the glass or nearby heating prevents the glass from dropping below the freezing point. When condensation forms readily, freezes, and is not melted by sufficient heat, it obscures the glass completely. Such a condition is not welcomed in any garden room.

The obscuring of the glass by frozen condensation can be prevented successfully by using double glazing. If two sheets of glass are separated by one quarter or one half an inch of space, the enclosed air acts as insulation. Hence such glazing is called *insulating glass*. It is more expensive than single glass of the same size, but it has advantages that are worth the price. First its insulating value cuts the heat loss of the room approximately in half and with it the consumption of fuel. Second, it allows higher humidities inside of a garden room before the condensation occurs. Third, it prevents the obscuring of glass with frozen moisture.

The effect of insulating glass on maintaining high inside humidities can be seen in this little example: if the outdoor temperature is 20° F and the garden room is maintained at 70° F, the condensation on single glass occurs at twenty-nine percent inside humidity or higher. On double glass, the moisture will start to condense at fifty-five percent inside humidity. If the outside temperature drops to 0° F the condensing on single glass will start at fifteen percent inside humidity (which is desert dry), but on the double glass condensation does not form only if the inside humidity is forty-two percent or more. Of course, the savings realized in fuel consumption by using double glass are greater than the advantages of frost-free glass.

A similar way should be followed when using plastic materials in place of glass. Plastics should be used for the roof only. The roof is not cleaned like the vertical glazing in a wall. The disadvantages of plastics is the ease with with which they are scratched or damaged with abrasive cleaners or solutions containing alcohol or solvents.

An all-glass enclosure for a garden room makes it possible to grow a very wide variety of plants by providing the greatest amount of daylight. However, this is not the only possible enclosure for a Room of Delight.

6
The Room with Solid Roof

Many plants available today are brought from tropical forests where they grow in dim light under a dense canopy of trees. Proper selection of such plants now makes possible a garden room without a glass roof. The large windows can supply enough light for the selected plants. Such a structure can be called the *enclosed porch type* construction and will make a satisfactory garden room. The suitable number of plants will be somewhat limited, especially in the flowering class, but still will allow a good selection. For this type of garden room can be used an existing porch or breezeway, properly adapted and equipped. First, all walls facing outside or to the garage must be insulated. Likewise the roof. It is best to use an insulation covered with foil or having a vapor barrier of asphalt paper, which should face the inside of the room, and then covered with desired wall or ceiling finish. Windows should be as large as possible and of insulating glass.

When a new enclosure of this type is built, it should rest on footings of proper depth to avoid frost heaving and consequent damage to the structure. Perimeter insulation should be installed next to the foundation walls to prevent cold floors and to save on heating cost. Perimeter insulation is especially important if ground beds are adjacent to the outside walls.

To provide extra light and effect, one or more skylights can be used. These will act as spotlights for a water fountain, special group of planting, or the seating area. A skylight can be easily installed even in existing roofs and is available in a wide variety of shapes: round, square, and rectangular. In this manner sufficient light can be provided in places where the light from windows cannot reach.

If the use of skylights can mean better and wider selection of plants, another device can provide more flowering plants. This device is called *window greenhouse*. Basically it is a window projected about sixteen inches away from the wall, all sides made of glass and equipped with glass shelves. A window greenhouse can be used as a single unit or several units can be combined. The view through such a window will be blocked somewhat by plants, but a window greenhouse can be located where vistas are not available anyway.

The garden room with solid roof is very economical not only to build, but also to heat. The absence of large glass roof areas means smaller heat loss and consequently a smaller heating bill. With proper plant selection the garden room of this type can be as enjoyable as the garden room of the conservatory type.

7

Heating of the Garden Room

The only reason that tropical plants can survive in a garden room during a severe winter is that there is a sufficient supply of heat. In this manner the exotic plants are like people, who cannot live in a freezing climate without heat. However, a difference exists between people and plants exposed to the frost: people can survive frost but tropical plants cannot. The *Episcias* from the family *Gesneriad* (relatives of African violets) are so sensitive to the lower temperatures that many die even when the temperature is above freezing. To many *Episcias* the temperature of 55° F is fatal, although some of them can survive 45° F. Heat is crucial for tropical plants.

Since the first orangeries were built, the heating systems for indoor gardens went through many changes. From free-standing cast-iron furnaces, needing an attendant day and night, to our simple and reliable systems was a long way. Today we enjoy the benefits of good, clean, fully automatic systems that are not only attendant free, but also relatively cheap.

What kind of heating should be used for the garden room? The answer can be narrowed down to two systems: hot water and warm air. Fin tube radiation, with a pump circulating hot water through pipes between the boiler and exact location where heat is needed, represents the best and most reliable system. It is more expensive than hot air, but it has advantages not available in other systems: gentle heat does not scorch or dry out plants which can be grown next to the heating enclosure; it is very quiet, so quiet it is hard to tell if the heat is on.

The heat has to be supplied where the heat loss occurs. Since the glass areas allow more heat to escape than solid walls, the heat is mostly supplied at the windows, although not exclusively. If the garden room enclosure is of the lean-to type, and has a light transmitting roof, then the heat also has to be supplied along the interior wall to combat heat losses through the roof.

Similar rules of heat distribution apply to the warm air system. In such a system the room air is sucked by a fan into a furnace, heated there, and discharged by the same blower into the room. The distribution of air is done by ducts, carrying and releasing air where needed.

The boiler or furnace should be located in some adjacent room or in the basement. Provisions should be done in the design stages for ducts or pipes to enter the garden room and for routing of the same, so the heat can be supplied where necessary.

Many small, hobby greenhouses are heated by warm air without ducts. It is done by a wall heater, recessed in the wall. The wall heater must be installed in the outside wall, since the air for combustion is taken from outside, and also smoke is discharged to the outside. One or two small fans in the heater circulate the room air through the heater and release it back to the room. If such a wall heater is used in a garden room, care must be taken that no plants are in the path of the hot air, blown from the heater. In the greenhouse a wall heater is generally located below the potting benches, where there are no plants, so the problem is not present.

To guard against unwanted drop in temperature, a low temperature alarm should be installed. Temperature drop can be caused by failure of the heating system, interruption of electricity supply, or malfunction of the automatic ventilator. An alarm consists of a battery, bell, and a thermostat set at 40° - 50° F. All components can be purchased in any large hardware store. Wiring is very simple. The low temperature alarm should be tested several times during the heating season to find if battery is active or wiring in order. Testing is done by moving the set point on the thermostat to the actual or higher temperature of the garden room. When the setting of the thermostat matches the actual temperature, the alarm bell should start ringing. After testing, the thermostat should be set down to the range of 40° - 50° F again.

Regardless of the type of heating system used, the garden room should have its own heating system, not connected with that of the house—unless it can be put on its own zone with separate controls. The lower night temperature—60° F— is very important to the plants and necessary for many of them to induce the bud setting and duration of flowering stage.

The location of the thermostat is also important. It must not be located on the outside wall, above fin tube radiation or warm air register. Such location will cause erratic functioning of the heating system and would not be capable of responding to the actual temperature requirements of the garden room.

A note on the insulating value of curtains: it is advantageous to pull the curtains for night in winter. The air enclosed between the glass and curtains provides an additional insulation, thus reducing the heat loss through the windows and with it provides saving of fuel.

8
Shading, Ventilating, and Cooling

Many older public conservatories do not have any mechanical ventilation or summer cooling. Yet inside is a bearable climate in the summer, a little warmer and more humid than outside. Such a comfortable climate is due to the huge size of these structures. The volume of air is large, and the difference between the cooler air inlet near the ground and ventilators in the apex of the dome provides a fast rate of air exchange.

Home conservatories do not have such an advantage. The volume of air is small and the natural ventilation insufficient. Even watering of the floor does not improve the situation. The solution is in mechanical cooling.

The build-up of heat in a garden room is due to the large glass areas. In winter or in cold weather of other seasons during sunshine, this fact is a great asset, since it reduces the heating load. On a cold winter day, if the sun is shining, the temperature inside our garden room is 70° F or more, without heating, even if outside it is —20° F. If such day occurs in late February, we have to pull the shades, because the sun gets stronger and burns.

Sun in winter is welcomed. It means free heat and better growth of plants. The same heat of the sun in summer causes problems of too much heat in any covered garden. Many commercial greenhouses solve it by simply emptying the greenhouse. Such a solution is not applicable to the garden room, because we want to use it year around.

Fortunately the excessive heat in a garden room can be prevented with the help of shading and removed by cooling. Shading of the vertical glass windows is simple. Any curtain in white or very light color, open weave and if possible of fiberglass, will do the job. The ease of opening and closing of curtains makes them very efficient and inexpensive shading.

Sometimes greenhouse owners and even commercial growers claim they do not need shading of greenhouses in the summer. It is possible because the need of shading the greenhouses depends on the locality. Near the sea coast or in the industrial areas smoke or water vapor is present in the air. The quantities of water vapor or smoke are so large that they reduce the sunshine and its heat by twenty-five percent or more.

To shade the clear glass roof is not as easy as to shade the windows. The problem of shading the roof can be eliminated by using milky or gray-colored glass, Plexiglas or fiberglass, with a light reduction of thirty to sixty percent. You cannot see the sky but the problem of shading the roof is eliminated. If a view of the sky and moonshine in the garden room is desired, then the clear roof must be shaded.

The old proven method of roof shading are the heavy bamboo shades, which are rolled up and down on the roof—outside; perhaps still the best of the shading, although quite expensive, since the replacement is necessary in a few years. The easiest and very economical are roller shades installed inside, just below the roof, the same type of roller shades used for windows. Regular shades, sold in department stores, generally can extend only four to six feet, but rollers with capacities to extend twelve to sixteen feet are available from firms specializing in floor covering and curtains. Rollers should be installed at the lower portion of the roof, at windows, and extended up to the high roof as the sun rises high in the sky. Since the shades extended horizontally have the tendency to sag, guides are available that will hold the fabric on the sides to prevent it from sagging.

Although the shading is installed in the garden room for reduction of heat, it is also necessary in providing shade for tropical plants, most of which cannot tolerate direct sun. Yet shading itself does not solve the problem of heat build-up in a garden room. Ventilation, or preferably cooling, is needed.

The ventilation has to be included in the design of the garden room enclosure. The precut greenhouse structures incorporate ventilators at the top of the roof and glass louvered windows and doors. In an independent design, or the "covered porch" type enclosure, ventilation must also be provided. Glass louvered windows are generally operated manually. Ventilators on top of the roof can also be manual, but often are opened and closed by electric motors, which can do it on command of thermostat or switch. The thermostatic control of ventilators is especially valuable in connection with the cooling.

The cooling of a garden room is achieved by an evaporative cooler. It is a very simple piece of equipment: a blower enclosed in a steel cabinet, walls of which are lined on three sides by aspen wood pads. The blower draws the air through the pads, which are continually wetted by water supplied by a small pump in the bottom of the cabinet. As the air passes through the wet pads, some of the water is evaporated. The water can evaporate only if heat is applied. The heat for evaporation of the water in the pads is taken from the air passing through the pads. In this way, the temperature of the passing air drops. The cooler air, together with water vapor, is discharged by the blower into the garden room.

Since the evaporative cooler uses large quantities of outside air, it has to be installed outside on the wall of the garden room, and to blow the air through an opening in the wall. Electricity and water supply has to be piped to the cooler through the wall. The action of the evaporative cooler is more effective if it blows the length of the room. Whenever the cooling is on, the ventilator at the far end of room must be opened. The air is not being recirculated. After it passes through the room it is pushed out. It is very important to keep closed all windows and ventilators near the cooler, even those high at the roof. Otherwise the air discharged from the cooler will draw through the open windows the hot air from outside and the cooling effect will be reduced, because not all air flowing into the room is being cooled.

The effectiveness of the evaporative cooler depends on two factors: the temperature and humidity of outside air. High temperature and low humidity give the optimum cooling. If, for example, the temperature outside is 90°F and humidity is 50 percent, the air through the cooler will drop 12°F. However if the humidity is only 20 percent at the same 90°F outside temperature, the air will be cooled almost 30°F. For this reason, evaporative cooling is used extensively in arid areas of the Southwest in residential and commercial air conditioning.

Evaporative cooling is far superior to the other forms of ventilation. For one reason, all air supplied to the garden room is filtered in the wet pads. The increased humidity of the air caused by the evaporation of water is very beneficial to the tropical plants that can stand high temperature but that lose vigor and fail to bloom in continued low humidities.

It is best when the evaporative cooler is controlled by a thermostat. There is no need to buy an extra one if the heating-cooling type is purchased, which can control heating as well as cooling. Another feature of the cooler comes in handy: the two-speed motors of the blower. It can be switched to the low speed in spring and fall when the full capacity of evaporative cooler is not needed. In installing the cooler on the wall, rubber washers should be placed between the wall and the cabinet of the cooler to prevent transmission of vibration and its noise.

The evaporation of water leaves deposits of solids (dissolved in water) in the pads, slowly clogging them and reducing the effectiveness. Depending on the hardness of the water, aspen wood pads have to be replaced after one or several seasons of operation.

Allophyton mexicanum

Manettia inflata

Dipladenia sanderi 'Rosea'

Acalypha 'Ceylon'

The water supply to the cooler should be insulated to prevent dripping and has to be shut off before the frost. Water must be drained from the pipe leading to the cooler. This can be easily done using a stop and waste valve. After the water is shut off, a small port is opened on the valve, which allows draining of water from the section of pipe between the valve and cooler.

The necessity of shading, ventilating, and cooling appears if the garden room faces south or west. The garden room oriented north does not need any, and the one facing east needs only some shading and ventilating. However, if you try to build a garden room so as to avoid the sun, you are robbing it of the brilliance, cheerfulness, and radiance that only the sun can give.

9
The Humidity

In a garden room where the temperature is 70°F and humidity 55 to 65 percent it is very comfortable to stay. If you enter into the house proper, which has a temperature of 72°F and humidity of 30 to 40 percent you suddenly feel cold. Your first reaction is: at least 10°F difference. Is the thermostat set correctly?

This phenomenon is easily explained. The human body continually gives off moisture that evaporates into the air. Any evaporation requires heat, which must be taken from our body. If the evaporation is faster, we feel cooler; if it is slow, we feel warmer. In the dry air the evaporation is faster and we feel cooler, even if the temperature is high. Humid air slows down our evaporation and we feel warmer.

Plants are living beings and are subjected to the same evaporation process as people. In fact, plants evaporate about 90 percent of water taken in. The faster the rate of evaporation, the more the plant has to "work" and is more exhausted—just like people get exhausted by working and sweating.

The high humidity, which retards evaporation, is beneficial to people as well as to plants. The exceptions are Cacti and some succulents living in areas of low humidity. These plants are protected from high evaporation by a tight and waxy surface, reducing the evaporation to the minimum. Tropical plants do not have such protection and require high humidity as a retardant of evaporation and security from "overworking."

Every garden room with tropical plants needs high humidity for the benefit of plants and people. The source of humidity varies with the layout of the garden room. In the "naturalistic" design, where all floor is soil except the walks, the damp soil itself is a sufficient source of humidity. Since the soil is kept moist, its drying, or evaporating, supplies enough humidity to the garden room.

When the design of the garden room is a "formal" one with the floor just like any other room of the house, then the humidity has to be supplied artificially. This is done easily with a humidifier—not a fancy or special one, but the simple, console type, sold in many stores, which supplies humidity by evaporating the water. A small fan draws the air from the room and blows it through the pads constantly wetted by water. Generally the operation of the fan and pump is automatic, controlled by a humidistat within the cabinet.

A humidifier is a good piece of equipment. Besides supplying humidity it also provides air movement and filters the air. Like any equipment it requires maintenance. After several months of operation it should be drained and pads washed in detergent and rinsed. The frequency of cleaning depends on the quality of water. Hard water requires more frequent cleaning: more solids are deposited in the pads and in the pan at the bottom. Even if the solids are not noticeable in the pan, water is saturated and the efficiency of the humidifier drops.

Some humidifiers do not vaporize water, but atomize it and discharge it as a stream of fine mist. The tiny droplets vaporize in the air. The water vapor is dispersed, but the solids dissolved in the water cannot, neither can they stay in the air. After some time of operation, yellowish or brownish "fallout" starts to cover everything in the room and is impossible to remove. The atomizing type of humidifier (sometimes called *cold mist*) can be operated successfully only with distilled or demineralized water of high purity (30 to 50 cents per gallon).

During summer months, especially during the intense sunshine, the humidity in the garden room will drop during the day down to 20 percent or even less. However, in the evening and at night it will rise again. Such variations of humidity are normal in subtropical and some tropical climates. Only in the tropics where it rains daily humidity remains continually high.

To know the humidity in the garden room is desirable. A combination thermometer-hygrometer is inexpensive and can be set on a table or hung on the wall (not the outside wall).

One phenomenon of winter humidification is the inability to maintain high humidity when outdoor temperature is very low. At -10° or -20°F the highest humidity in the garden room will be about 50 percent since the moisture condenses faster than the humidifier can produce it.

A somewhat similar situation exists on windy days, with winds blowing at high velocities. Such winds suck out with the air also the water vapor from the garden room, and the humidity falls down to the 20 to 30 percent range.

In order to maintain high humidity, the doors and windows should be closed. In hot weather, when ventilation is necessary, the humidity will drop rapidly, unless an evaporative cooler is in operation. In fall, winter and spring when all vents are closed, it is easy to maintain high humidity; the water vapor, which is humidity, cannot escape.

A commercial greenhouse does not have humidity problems. Benches are watered daily, the soil is continually saturated, and the humidity is high. Such a condition is not likely to be found in a garden room, especially if the floor is concrete or stone. To have a concrete floor is not such a handicap as it might seem. In that case a humidifier is a necessity. But it has a dual purpose: it provides humidity and also air movement. The still, humid air supports the growth of mold and fungi. Commercial growers combat this problem by installing a fan which circulates air within the greenhouse and distributes it through a long, plastic tube full of openings. In a garden room a humidifier does the same.

10

Heating in Emergency

Our heating systems are safe and reliable. However, all heating installations hang on the wire that supplies them with electricity. Any downing of wires or power failure makes the best heating system inoperative. Similarly, each system can be shut down by a breakdown of some component, be it a pump, motor or some control. However, the old-fashioned fireplace and a pile of wood can save plants from freezing and pipes from bursting. Oh yes, you have to babysit the flame and keep loading wood to maintain a large fire supplying sufficient heat.

Once I had to do it all night when after nine o' clock in the evening, the oil pump stopped functioning. It happened just at the time when the outdoor temperature dropped to —10°F. The large fire in the fireplace kept the temperature in the garden room at 55°F. A small electric heater was set in the center of room and the door to the house was opened to provide more heat. Even when toward morning the temperature dropped to 50°F, the heat sensitive Episcias did not rebel by dropping their leaves and going dormant.

An alternative to the fireplace for emergencies is a tent heater, also called catalytic heater. It burns white gasoline without an open flame and is harmless to plants. The heating capacity of a tent heater is rather small, and for a larger garden room several would be required. On one fill it will burn for about ten hours.

Regardless of the type, some emergency heat should be provided for the garden room.

11
Lights in the Garden Room

Many short-day plants must have complete darkness or very low levels of illumination for setting the buds. Light, even for a very short period, can prevent setting of buds of: Christmas cactus, *Poinsettia, Chrysanthemum,* Christmas pepper, and *Euphorbia fulgens.* If lights are of very low intensity, it is possible to enjoy the flowering of Christmas cactus, *Poinsettias,* and *Chrysanthemums* until April or May.

In order to achieve this, some simple precautions are necessary. One light fixture for our garden room has a switch in the adjacent room. The regular bulb was replaced with a deep green 60-watt bulb, which gives light of moonshine intensity. It is sufficient to see plants, even to water them, but it does not disturb the setting of buds, even if someone leaves it on all night.

The general illumination in our garden room is furnished by four light fixtures hanging from beams. These are made of colored glass chips; likewise, the removable plate in the bottom. The bulbs are only 25 watts. The light filtered through red, blue, green, and yellow pieces is very subdued. Directly under the lamps, 24 inches above the floor, the intensity of light is only 0.7 of a footcandle. Such intensity is below the limit preventing the setting of the buds. The most sensitive poinsettia will not set buds if the shining light has an intensity of 1.5 footcandle or more.

The stained-glass lamps proved very successful in our garden room. In addition to supplying reduced light, the colored glass lamps provide a special mood not achieved with plain bulbs or plastic shades.

12
The Soothing Sound of Water

The subdued sound of moving water has a soothing effect on human nerves. To rest next to a bubbling brook is very refreshing, even if few people would have a gurgling stream running through their bedroom, as the king Dionysios in Syracuse, on Sicily, had in the fourth century B.C.

The pools and fountains jetting streams of water into the air became an indispensable part of the garden layout of Roman gardens. Because we owe our designs of gardens to the Roman example, the gardens of our times have fountains and pools also.

The concept of water among plants was transferred into the indoor gardens. Today it is hard to find a conservatory without mirrors of pools and the soothing sounds of splashing water. If no garden room is complete without a pool or fountain, it is so because in nature the most beautiful areas have still or running water.

The pool in the garden room can be of any size and shape. Ours is a triangle with sides six feet long and a curved front. I arrived at this shape, to gain the greatest possible use of floor area.

The pool in the garden room can be resting on the floor, elevated, or sunken. Materials used are: concrete, fiberglass, or artificial stone. Some can be purchased ready made, often with ornaments and statuettes. If concrete is used in construction of the the garden pool, it has to be sealed; concrete itself is not impervious to water. Two coats of epoxy paint applied within 24 hours will make it water tight. Epoxy paint has to be cured for at least seven days before filling the pool with water. Such a paint job will be good for about five years. Before repainting, the old paint has to be well scuffed with coarse sandpaper or a steel brush.

Each pool should have some provision for drainage. This is very important, especially when the pool is larger or sunken in the floor. Small pools, containing a few gallons of water, are easily drained into a bucket. It is possible to empty a larger pool with a small pump, discharging into the sink. The best is to have the drain connected to the house sewer. Then the draining of the pool is done easily by lifting a lever or removing a stopper.

Jets of water are powered by a small and simple pump. Many pumps for pools are made of plastic and therefore are very cheap. On the contrary, some fountain heads distributing water in complicated patterns are more expensive than the plastic pump. Quite touchy are the spray rings, having numerous small jets. The small openings plug easily not only because of some impurities in the pool water but in areas of hard water, the high content of minerals in the water will slowly choke off the small openings in the spray ring by mere evaporation of the flowing water.

Many spray heads are available, designed to form creative patterns of rising and falling water. Such sprays are especially effective in pools without statuettes. Where small statues are used in the pool or around, it is better to stress their presence by jets of water discharging from various parts of the statue itself. Often statuettes intended for use in the garden are equipped with holes for small diameter pipe or have the pipe already installed.

Fountain in Room of Delight.

Garden statues sold by some nurseries or specialized studios are mostly copies of some famous contemporary or historical statues. The price is governed by their size and material. The least expensive are made from artificial stone. The most costly are from statuary bronze. The price of other materials, like lead and carved stone, is in-between. The garden statues are heavy, except the very small ones. Good anchoring is necessary to prevent accidental toppling and injury.

If you plan to have a fountain, that is any movement of water in the garden pool, you cannot grow any aquatic plants. Lotus and water lilies must have calm water, although a very slow exchange of water is necessary to prevent formation of a swampy condition. But even the pool with aquatic plants has to be cleaned at least once a year.

Slightly more and easier maintenance is required for the pool with a fountain. The problem with any body of water is algae, which grow rapidly, and movement of water does not disturb them. Fortunately, algae are fairly easy to control. The most simple and cheapest way is the application of chlorine. Doses depend on the strength of the solution. The easiest is the laundry bleach, ¾ cup for 100 gallons of pool volume, applied every week. If the slight odor of chlorine does not annoy you when the pump is operating, then the chlorine treatment is the easiest and is quite effective, provided the application is made weekly.

Another algaecide is copper sulphide, obtainable from the drugstore. Two ounces per 100 gallons of pool volume every week will keep algae under control. However, children must be prevented from reaching and playing in the pool for 24 hours after application. The other objection to copper sulphide is the cloudiness of the water, which stays milky for several days.

No matter which algaecide is used, it cannot completely prevent the growth of algae. After several weeks it is necessary to empty the pool, scrub it with a good cleaner, and refill it with fresh water.

13
Organic Gardening?

At present organic gardening is becoming fashionable. By that I meant the use of only natural fertilizers, provided by composting and decaying of other vegetative remnants, and the controlling of insects by predators, without the use of poisonous insecticides.

Both concepts are easily put in practice in outdoor gardens, and are older than the human race. These concepts are nature's ways, always present in a balanced eco-system. The balanced eco-system is becoming a rarity, apparent today only in large rain forests (jungles) of the tropical regions or in natural and large forests and prairies of the temperate zones. Large forests and swamps provide their own fertilizer from decaying vegetative parts; prey is controlled by predators and vice versa. When prey diminishes the predators control their own offspring either by limited reproduction or by depriving the young ones of food. The prey — which means food — is always kept in sufficient numbers by predators. The balanced eco-system can also support a limited amount of people, as it was with American Indians not long ago, and still is going on with small native tribes of jungle people.

Large concentrations of people require more food and production of specific crops only. Production of any food for men and animals removes large quantities of certain minerals from the soil. These must be replenished if productivity of the soil is to be maintained. Intensive cultivation removes such quantities of minerals from the soil that chemical fertilizers are the only answer.

Similarly disturbed is the balance between insects and their predators in any unbalanced eco-system. Certain crops support numbers of insects, whereas their predators are few, perhaps because of insufficient protection. So, the insecticides have to be put into use to control the prevalent insect.

The great majority of mankind live in unbalanced eco-systems. We must accept this fact and its consequences. Not even the most forceful promoter of organic gardening would like to have many apples wormy, or to eat bread and pastry whose taste is spoiled by scab or ergots in the wheat. Nobody likes to buy deformed bananas or lettuce with slimy slugs. The abundant, clean, and healthy foods we enjoy today are the products of chemical fertilizers and frequent applications of insecticides.

Any garden room is an unbalanced eco-system of first class. You can start with your garden room in early spring or late fall, when outdoors there is no insect activity—only to discover later that many plants are infested with spider mites, aphids, mealy bugs, or the white fly. These very small insects can always find large enough cracks to enter the enclosure in pursuit of the attractive smell of fresh plants. Their predators, like lady bugs or ants, being much larger, are excluded by the enclosure.

Even if we would introduce predators into the garden room they never would eliminate their prey completely. It is nature's law that predators always leave certain amount of prey to preserve their own food supply. Only man eliminates his enemies completely. The elimination of insects in our protective environments of greenhouses and garden rooms is possible only with the help of insecticides.

The same applies to the fertilizers. If we give to our plants the precious space, protected and heated, we want from them production of blossoms and foliage. That is the plant's payment for our care and effort. To support production of our protected plants, we must give them necessary nutrients. The introduction of manure and compost into the garden room is out of the question. Not only would we introduce more insects and weeds—and so push to environment even more out of balance but the compost is slow acting in decomposition and the consequent release of the nutrients. Besides, the plants do not care at all where the necessary inorganic elements (salts of nitrogen phosphorus, potash, etc.) come from. Any plant is absolutely indifferent to the fact of where the needed building blocks of chemicals are derived from: organic manure, artificial fertilizer, or minerals in the soil.

The use of chemical fertilizers and insecticides in the garden room is nothing else but a practical answer to the unbalanced eco-system.

14
The Life-giving Light

The two greatest factors limiting the growth inside of home greenhouses are insufficient heat in winter and heavy shading in summer. Shading reduces heat build-up and with it light intensity. On sunny days enough light is supplied through the shades. However, heavy shading on cloudy days reduces the light intensity below the minimum level necessary for good growth.

The misunderstanding of the light requirements of plants is widespread. In the past, people knew that plants indoors need all the available light and tried to provide it. The old proverb, "without light is no life," was applied even to the house plants. Nowadays many are confused by interior decorators and home magazines picturing plants on odd places in the buildings where light cannot even reach. True, some decorators select plants for low light-level requirements like *Ficus, Dracaenas, Dieffenbachias,* and *Philodendrons*. Those plants grow in their locations well, generally benefiting from high illumination levels in offices or stores. Contrary to that, many plants in picture magazines are placed in odd locations just for making the photograph, and do not otherwise grow there. This creates the illusion, in many minds, that any plant will grow in any spot of any building.

Sufficient light is of utmost importance to every plant. Vegetation with green foliage manufactures its own food from carbon in the air and minerals in the soil, transported to the leaves by water. But the key, which makes possible the conversion of chemicals into sugars, is light. If light is not sufficient, not enough food is manufactured and the plant starves despite generous fertilizing and watering. The lush vegetation in the tropics is not only the result of warm temperature, abundance of moisture, and humidity. The light intensity on the equator is two and half times greater than on 50° latitude.

In any indoor garden, the light intensity is always lower than outdoor, due to the light transmission losses in building materials. However, the shading materials cut the light greatly. The curtains on the south wall of our garden room are off-white color, ⅛ inch open weave. The direct sunshine through them is reduced by sixty percent. It seems impossible to the eyes. Only careful measurement with a highly sensitive exposure meter reveals this fact.

15

The Necessities of Plants

Some friends coming to our garden room remarked several times: "You must take good care of your plants that they are doing so well." The fact is, we do not provide any extraordinary care. Naturally, plants get what is needed — but they are not pampered. Watering, which is most crucial, has to be done as each plant requires. However, the fertilizing is very modest.

In the minds of many people, fertilizing is the key to the success of growing plants. Nothing is further from the truth. The key to the success of growing any plant is proper environment. In an enclosed garden, proper environment is nothing more than duplicating nature's conditions. That means proper temperature, humidity, ventilation, and air movement. The importance of these has already been discussed. Other necessary requirements are soil, watering, fertilizing, and insect control.

Soil: The Growing Medium

Few aspects of gardening generate more discussion, controversy, and trials than the soil. Naturally, soil is important. But not so important that recipes for certain soils must be followed in order to have success.

Most plants can be grown in water or sand if nutrients are added regularly. On this fact is based the so called soilless gardening, popular a few decades ago. Basically, it means to add weak solutions of complete fertilizer to the water or sand daily or weekly. Plants will grow more rapidly but will not be better. Such gardening is more tedious, requiring more attention and also higher initial cost. Everything in contact with the fertilizer solution must be of noncorosive materials: stainless steel, plastics, or other materials coated with asphalt. Growing plants without soil has its value where controlled growth is necessary, like in a laboratory, where the concept of soilless gardening had its origin.

Gardening books, encylopedias, and magazines are always offering several recipes for soil mixtures. Some even say which mixture should be used for the particular plant. Although I recognize the need of certain plants for special soil mixtures, the majority of plants are not particular. For years I have used a very simple soil mixture: to the regular garden loam, or black dirt, is added 25 to 30 percent of sharp sand. The percentage is measured by volume, not by weight. This soil is good for almost all plants with little modifications where a plant has special requirements. *Poinsettias* and succulents want more sandy soil, so the sand content is increased to 50 percent. For *Cactus* even more sand is added, up to 70 percent. For *Azaleas* and other acid-loving plants peat moss is added — or they can be potted in peat moss only.

The sand in the soil is important to prevent caking and water logging, which ultimately would lead to rotting of the roots. Soil mixture with about 30 percent sand is fluffy and porous; from my experience plants must like it. Having only one soil mixture eliminates many problems, like storage of mixed soil and the confusion of which mix to use where.

Up to now I have not been talking about sterilized soil, because I do not use it. Such a statement might surprise some gardeners, but it is true. Sterilized soil is not necessary. The worst danger in not using sterilized soil are nematodes. In our area nematodes are not a problem, because the soil freezes to a depth of more than three feet. Freezing temperatures kill nematodes. To have more assurance I always store soil over the winter outside, to freeze it solid. It takes several days to thaw a container, but there is no rush.

To have mixed soil on hand is a great advantage. You never know when some plants are in need of repotting or when rooted cuttings need to be planted. To mix soil in large quantities is best. I mix it on the garage floor. First goes the black dirt, which is spread to the height of two to three inches. On top is spread sand; the actual mixing is done with a steel rake.

Any container for storage of mixed soil is suitable, as long as you can lift it either full or partly filled and move it to the storage area. I store it in a small room in the garage, where the boiler heating the garden room is. The boiler supplies enough heat even in the coldest weather, so I can repot plants any time. A small bench, some shelves, and a supply of pots make this working area complete. Next to the mixed soil stands a container of sand. It is used to fill the bottom of each pot first. About a half inch of sand in the bottom of pot prevents water from collecting and the roots from rotting. Of course, the drainage hole has to be covered first with a piece of broken clay pot or stone.

Even if you buy sterilized soil, it is advantageous to add sand. Many potting mixes have a very low percentage of perlite or vermiculite and cake easily. On the contrary, sand is very cheap from a sand pit or building-materials supplier.

Besides sterilized potting soil (black dirt), a number of soilless mixtures are available. Generally it is a combination of milled sphagnum moss and vermiculite sold under different names. Soilless mix is sterile and excellent for starting seeds and rooting of some cuttings. It is very light and not a welcomed potting soil for larger plants, which then topple easily.

Soilless mixture does not have any nutrients. Plants grown in such a medium can survive only with frequent applications of weak fertilizer. Every second or third watering should be done with weak fertilizer. By "weak" is meant a solution only one-fifth or one-sixth of the strength recommended as normal by the manufacturer. This recommendation is only an approximation based on practical experience. Growing plants in such an artificial medium has never been tested under laboratory conditions.

Fertilizers: Growth Promoters

Rich garden loam, mixed with sand, makes an excellent potting medium. It is possible to grow plants in it without any fertilizers. Repotting a plant two times a year will bring enough nutrients, if at each repotting fresh, rich soil is added. To avoid unnecessary repotting and work, fertilizers are used to replenish exhausted soil.

Today's fertilizers are clean, efficient, and simple to use. A great variety of them is available — liquid, powdered, and concentrated—in just about every combination of nutrients desired. The nutrient content is indicated by three numbers on the package. The numbers 15-30-15, for example, mean that the contents will provide the plants with 15 percent of nitrogen, 30 percent of phosphorus, and 15 percent of potash. These three chemicals are the basic building materials of any green plant. Nitrogen supports the growth of lush foliage; phosphorus promotes abundant blooming; potash builds a strong root system, firm stalks, and branches.

However, the rich, humusy soil has minute quantities of a number of chemicals, mostly salts of metals, that are necessary for proper growth. Any good fertilizer also contains small quantities, fractions of a percent, of boron, copper, iron, manganese, and zinc. If a fertilizer is missing the necessary minute quantities of metal, described either on the package or in an accompanying pamphlet, it is not recommended to use it—at least not for a prolonged period of time. Those fractions of a percent of iron, copper, etc. are the secret of making the plants perky. This is especially important where soil is not being changed, like in the ground beds or slow growing plants. The fertilizer containing small but necessary quantities of metals is called the *complete fertilizer*.

In selecting a fertilizer it is best to pick the one which has a nitrogen content lower than that of phosphorous and perhaps potash. A high percentage of nitrogen is good for growing grass. In a garden room it will cause rapid growth of foliage, fewer flowers, and spindly, elongated plants (although spindly plants can also be caused by insufficient light). Perhaps the best combination is 15-30-15, as Miracle-Gro has. Another reason for avoiding high nitrogen percentage fertilizers is its support of insects. A recent research revealed that it is harder to kill mites on plants grown in an abundance of nitrogen and potash.

How often should you fertilize? The manufacturer of a fertilizer wants you to use it every other week. His eagerness in applying fertilizer is understandable. On the other hand some people fertilize once in many long months. Both cases are extremes. Applying the fertilizer once in 4 to 6 weeks gives about the necessary nutrients to the plants in an indoor garden. In winter, this period can be extended by an additional 2 to 3 weeks, due to the low light levels and short days.

Sometimes you will hear of commercial growers fertilizing every week or every other week. Of course, they have their share of plants that succumb. Commercial producers of plants are naturally interested in rapid growth, so they can realize some profit. However, such heavy fertilizing is not as bad as it sounds. As soon as the plant leaves commercial greenhouses, it is put on a famine diet. Most people buying the plants do not fertilize at all, or after a long time, when it is discovered that the plant is not doing well.

One method of fertilizing should be mentioned: the foliar feeding. It still haunts many readers of garden magazines and is also recommended by some fertilizer manufacturers. Simply, it is a suggestion to fertilize plants by spraying their leaves with a fertilizer. In many tests this type of feeding proved void of any value. All that you get is spots on leaves when using wettable powder fertilizer. It is not worth the effort.

A number of plants have a greater need of iron. If the iron supply in the soil is exhausted, plants react to it by an inability to produce sufficient amounts of green coloring (chlorophyl). The result is leaves yellowing and falling off. Iron deficiency, called chlorosis, is easily corrected with chelated iron. Coming in the form of powder, it is mixed with water and applied at watering time. Application instructions should be followed carefully, since too strong or too much of iron chelate can easily kill smaller plants in the pot. Large plants or trees, especially if planted in ground beds, are not subjected to injury. The plants inclined to suffer from iron deficiency include: *Azalea, Camelia,* Citrus, Coffee, *Gardenia, Hibiscus, Geranium, Ixora,* Rose.

The coffee tree often develops leaves with yellowish streaks. Sometimes it can be corrected with an application of iron chelate. Sometimes, however, this treatment fails. Coffee needs much more potash than other plants. Often, the cure is to add to the soil either potash or fertilizer high in potash.

Water: The Lifeblood Of Vegetation

If it is easy to say how often to apply fertilizer, it is equally hard to say how often to water. Watering is complicated not only by different requirements of plants. The frequency of watering is also dictated by the conditions of the air.

Plants vary greatly in the intake of water. The *Philodendrons,* Ivy, *Zebrinas,* and *Strobilanthes* can grow luxuriantly in pots sitting in bowls of water. Such treatment would kill for sure *Cactus, Geraniums,* and Succulents. These are only few examples of the extremes of watering. The variable conditions of the air in the garden room only aggravate the situation.

To the plants, water is the vehicle for transportation of the basic elements of food. The greatest part of water—90 percent—is evaporated into the air. The rate of evaporation depends on sunlight, temperature, humidity, and air movement. Sunlight, high temperature, low humidity, and volumes of air moved by a fan forcing plants to "perspire" more, to evaporate more water. On such days, daily watering is necessary for the majority of plants; succulents will require watering every third day. When the sky is cloudy, temperature in garden room about 70°F, humidity 60 to 80 percent, and fan inoperative, then most of the plants will need water every second or third day; Succulents, *Geraniums,* and most *Begonias* will be satisfied if watered once a week, if such conditions prevail for several days.

The description of plants in this book indicates

the requirements of water for each plant.

MOIST SOIL: Keep it moist all the time. Such plants can even stand in a bowl of water and will perform admirably on wick watering.

MODERATELY MOIST: Water when top of soil is dry.

MODERATELY DRY: Plant should be left dry between waterings.

DRY: in hot summer, water twice a week; in winter, once a week.

This is only an approximate guide. After some time you will get to know your plants and acquire a feel for them; then your watering will be geared better to the requirements of each plant.

An easy way to know the requirements of plants is to provide each with a colored tag. The color code can be personal. A blue tag can mean: keep the plant moist; a red tag: keep dry. White tag or no tag indicates: water when top of soil is dry. Plastic tags are best. A tag can be a strip of plastic a half inch wide and 2 or 3 inches long, stuck into the pot at the rim. Disposable plastic bottles from household bleach offer plenty of material for such watering tags.

The temperature of the water is very important. Many people just draw water from the faucet and pour it into the pot. They do not realize that all indoor plants are tropicals, which very seldom, if ever, experienced a cold rain of 40-50° F in their natural habitat. Such water temperature gives thermal shock to the tropical plants and sets them back at each watering. Some plants can be killed by tap water in winter. The source of water of many cities is a river or lake. During a long and cold winter, the city water can have a very low temperature. In Minneapolis, Minnesota, the tap water in February flows at 36-38°F. The well water in northern parts of the United States is 50-55°F year round.

Very often you will read advice: for watering of house plants, use water at room temperature. For many people, that means to take a bucket, fill it with water and let it stand someplace for a time. The water temperature in the bucket is never the same as the room temperature. Everybody reads the temperature in his room from the thermostat mounted five feet above the floor. The floor, however, is always 5-10°F cooler than the air five feet above.

Researchers working with tropical plants are using water at 85°F for watering. The automatic temperature mixing valve performs the exact mixing by only opening the faucet. Few individuals will spend money for such a device. The majority of home gardeners will mix the hot and cold water directly and test its temperature. Testing can be done either by a thermometer or by your hand. The body surface temperature is 84°F with slight variations between the young and older people. Any temperature below 84°F feels cold and above 84°F feels warm. If the water is at body temperature, then a hand does not feel either cold or warm. Of course, if you want to be exactly on 85°F, then the thermometer is the answer. But it will not work when the garden hose is used for watering.

The fastest watering is with a garden hose and a special attachment. The hose has to be connected to a mixing faucet with hot and cold water, to have tempered water of approximately 85°F. At the other end is screwed on a watering attachment, consisting of a handle, an operating valve, and an aluminum tube 36 inches long. The valve of the attachment is normally closed, opening only with the squeeze of the handle. The greater the pressure on the handle, the more the valve opens. In this way it is possible to control the water from a trickle to full flow. The long tube brings water exactly to any pot on the floor, shelf, or hanging basket. This type of watering is especially appreciated in watering of the ground beds, always requiring large quantities of water. It is also very useful in outdoor watering, since it brings water directly to the roots. The special watering attachment is available from Bete Fog Nozzle Co. It is called "brush sprayer" by the manufacturer.

A very different type of watering is wick watering.

Wick Watering

A number of plants need large quantities of water for proper growth and development. If the soil is continually wet, they do not mind; in fact, they love it. It is hard to satisfy them with regular watering, since the rate of water evaporation through the leaves is much greater than that of the other plants. Such plants are best satisfied with wick watering.

Wick watering is based on the principle of capillary action: the dry soil will attract moisture from moist soil or from a water reservoir. If the connection between the soil and the reservoir is made of long fibers, the dry soil will draw water from the container as needed.

Several systems were devised. One uses a long section of nylon or fiberglass rope. One end is firmly tucked in the soil of the pot. The other end is submerged in a container of water standing next to the flower pot. This system has the advantage in that it does not excessively waterlog the soil. The disadvantage is in too much space taken by the container of water standing next to the plant.

The original wick watering system, developed by professor Kenneth Post of Cornell University, has the water container below the flower pot. The wick is much shorter, extending from the bottom of the pot to the bottom of the water reservoir. Such an arrangement has the advantage of not taking much more space than the pot itself. The disadvantage is making the soil in the pot quite wet, if the water reservoir is kept full of water. For some plants this is a necessity; for others it is better to leave the container empty for a few days after a week or two.

The wick watering arrangement is not elaborate. The wick itself must be of material that will not deteriorate. Nylon, fiberglass rope, or cloth is best. The rope can be substituted by a tube made from fabric. A three-by-five-inch section of nylon or fiberglass is rolled into a tube five inches long, about a quarter inch thick, and held together with nylon thread. If rope is available, it is easily cut into five inch sections. A one-inch length of one end, either rope or tube, is then frayed into a circle; the tube has to be cut into several 1-¼-inch-long sections, which are bent back to form a star. The wick is then inserted through the drainage hole of the pot (from inside). The frayed section inside of the pot is covered with a half inch of sand, firmed well with the hand. The layer of soil follows next, also tamped down firmly. The plant is then planted in the pot in the usual way, compressing the soil around the roots. In tamping of soil and sand is the secret of wick watering. Before the water can be drawn from the reservoir it must have the continuity of compacted soil.

For a water container, a bowl of any kind can be used: cereal or soup bowls molded at home from Plexiglas or fiberglass, or any glazed pottery. Plastic and ceramic bowls are preferred to the metal. Any bowl used as a water reservoir is then topped with a section of ¼-inch galvanized wire mesh, which holds the pot above the bowl. An opening cut into the center of the wire mesh lets the wick slide through easily.

Wick watering makes it possible to go away for one week in the hot summer, without leaving somebody in care of the plants. It is, however, not widely accepted, because nobody had published a list of plants suitable for this type of watering. Only African violets have been recommended. To find which plants are suitable for wick watering, I tested 125 plants. To gain more reliable results, the reservoir was never empty. The test was run for six months, although many plants are still on wick after three years.

The plants well suited for wick watering are:
Aeschynanthus 'Black Pagoda'
Aphelandra squarrosa

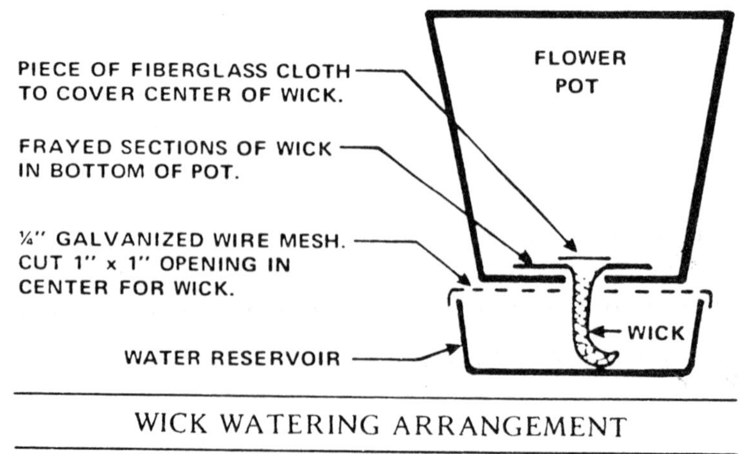

WICK WATERING ARRANGEMENT

Begonias: boweri 'Bow Chancee'
boweri 'Nigra Marga'
convolvulacea
fuscomaculata
ricinifolia
Browallia speciosa
Capsicum annuum
Coleus
Columneas: 'Early Bird' 'Cornelian'
Chrysanthemums
Dracaena marginata
Ervatamia coronaria
Ficus stricta
Gynura tomentosa
Impatiens sultanii
Iresine herbstii
Neomarica gracilis
Pentas lanceolata
Philodendron hastatum
Plectranthus oertendahlii
Poinsettia
Rhoeo discolor
Saintpaulias
Sanchesia nobilis
Setcreasea pallida
Strobilanthes dyerianus
Syngonium podophyllum
Tradescantias
Zebrinas

Several of these plants, like *Coleus, Iresine,* and *Strobilanthes,* require large quantities of water, and the best way to prevent them from wilting is to keep water in reservoir all the time.

Some everblooming plants grew well on the wick, but stopped blooming. This happened with wax *Begonias, Lantana montevidensis,* and *Bougenvilleas.*

A number of plants performed well for a period of time from six weeks to six months: *Clerodendrum thompsonae, Dieffenbachia* 'Rudolph Roehrs', *Hibiscus rosa sinensis, Maranta erythroneura, Spathiphyllum* 'Mauna Loa,' *Epiphyllum cactus.*

Unsuitable proved *Geraniums, Begonia cathayna,* rex *Begonias.* Also unsuitable are succulents and many plants recommended to be grown dry.

Obviously other plants can be found acceptable for wick watering. The list of plants given here are only those which I tested myself.*

*Lists of plants suitable and unsuitable for wick watering, together with other pertinent data, were published by author in March and April 1970 issues of *The Begonian.* Reprinted with permission

16
Plant Propagation Methods

Each plant must perpetuate in order to survive. In fact, the reason why many plants are so loved by people is their propagating machinery — the blossoms. In open nature, propagation is aided by wind, insects and birds, although some plants are self-pollinating. The garden room enclosure shuts out these propagation aids, again proving how unbalanced an eco-system any enclosed garden is.

The perpetuation of plants in a garden room depends on its owner. Pollination is used mostly when fruit is desired. For pollinating of citrus and coffee blossoms a soft brush is very useful. The Jerusalem cherry and Christmas peppers are self-pollinating, although occasional shaking of the plant (as with tomatoes) will result in a greater percentage of fruit.

Aside from hybridizing, pollination for seed production is very limited in any garden room. The raising of plants from seeds is quite a long process, compared with other means of propagation. The fastest and safest way is vegetative propagation. Many plants propagate from soft-stem cuttings, some from half-ripened wood, and again others from ripened woody sections of the stem. The most admirable propagation is from the sections of the leaf. Plants having rhizomes propagate from its sections. Some plants form little offshoots or bulbils and in this way provide us with new plants. Another very easy way is layering and air layering.

Growing from Seeds

Propagation from seeds is the most common one in nature. It is also used for raising the plants for an indoor garden. Plant societies sell seeds of rare plants, not available in commerce. It is therefore advantageous to know how to raise seedlings.

For germination of seeds, the use of a sterile medium is imperative. When ordinary, unsterilized soil is used, the small seedling is generally seized and ruined by damping-off. The damping-off is mold, which grows in the protective environment of seedlings very fast and finally, as parasites, overtakes the seedling. The best sterile medium for seedlings is milled sphagnum moss and its combinations, sold under different trade names (Ready Mix; Jiffy Mix). These mixes are fluffy, not caking when soaked with water. The sterile medium cannot be reused for another seed starting, since it loses its sterility with the use of nonsterile water. However it can be used as an admixture in potting soil, where it performs perfectly.

The sterile medium is put in a container, which should be clean, free from any foreign deposits and contamination. Plastic or glass containers are best, provided they have a drain opening in the bottom. The container is filled with the sterile medium and well watered. After waiting a half an hour, and with excess water drained away, it is ready for sowing. (The water used for soaking does not have to be distilled water.)

With the seeding of the seeds the question always comes up: To cover or not to cover the seeds? The answer is the size of the seeds. The dustlike seeds (*Begonias, Gesneriads*) are only sprinkled on top of the seeding medium, without being covered. Larger seeds are covered with the same thickness of seeding medium as is the diameter of the seed. This is a rule of thumb, which normally works well. Packages of seeds bought from commercial growers carry instructions. The plant societies do not have instructions printed on their seed packages, but have available pamphlets on propagation of their plants.

When the seeds are seeded, the container should be covered with a piece of clear glass or plastic. Better yet, slip the container into a clear plastic bag and close tight, so moisture cannot escape. The slow evaporation of water saturating the sterile medium creates the high humidity necessary for good germination. The enclosed container should be put in a place where there is good light, but not direct sun, and not too warm (like next to the heating radiation or register). Sun should never shine on an enclosed container with seeds germinating, which is like a miniature greenhouse. Sunshine would rapidly raise the temperature of the enclosed air even as high as 100° F. Such a temperature is always fatal to the germinating seeds and seedlings.

The seeds of tropical plants need continuous warmth for germination. Since the temperature in the garden room is always reset for night down to 60° F, the garden room is not the ideal place to keep germinating seeds. The exception would be the use of electric heating cable with built-in or adjustable thermostat, to maintain the temperature in the seed bed at 70° F or higher. The seeds will germinate in any other room in good light. In the summer, the temperature in our house is above 70° F and in winter is generally kept at 70° F even at night. Many of my seeds germinated on the television set, which gives additional heat when turned on.

After many seeds germinate, the plastic bag should be partly opened to provide access to the air. If glass or plastic was used for covering of the container, it should be shifted and let the air circulate over the tiny seedlings. The transplanting should not be rushed. Seedlings always find little nourishment in a sterile medium. It is best to wait with transplanting until the second set of the tiny leaves grows. Similarly it is better to wait with fertilizing. Transplanted seedlings have plenty of nourishment in the rich soil and do not need fertilizer for 6 to 8 weeks; even then a weak solution of fertilizer should be used. The regular strength of fertilizer might burn the hairlike roots.

The small seedlings should be placed in the garden room to have enough light but not direct sun. Insufficient light will cause them to grow tall and spindly.

Propagation from Cuttings

Cuttings are used for creating new plants fast. For hybrid plants, it is necessary to use this or another way of vegetative propagation, if the hybrid plant has to perpetuate without reverting to one of the parents.

The most common way of cutting propagation is rooting in water. It is a simple way, without much fuss, frequently used. It works well with a large number of plants, especially with soft cuttings, and is equally successful for many woody cuttings. Some people attempt to root cuttings of any plant in water. And they are strengthened in their attempts by the amazing ability of the plants. Many plants require dry soil for proper growth; continually moist soil will cause stem rot. However cuttings of the same plant will root in the water. Wax *Begonia* and Jade plant are good examples.

Generally, plants having soft stems and branches are good candidates for rooting cuttings in water (*Coleus*, wax *Begonias*, *Zebrinas*). Many plants with semihardy stems will root in water also — even bloom there. The cane-type *Begonias* and *Philodendrons* lead the other plants in this manner.

Even if the rooting of cuttings in water is simple and fast, it is not the easiest way for the plant itself. The roots grow fast in water, but when the rooted cutting is transplanted into the pot, it does not grow fast. The reason for this is, that the roots grown in the water have to be replaced by new roots, before the plant can start the normal growth.

All cuttings rooting successfully in water will root also in some other medium. Just about a universal one is clean, sharp sand, which will promote good root growth without stem rot. The excessive water drains easily away and, at the same time, enough is retained to prevent rapid drying. Some plants requiring a high degree of moisture, like

Azalea or *Strobilanthes*, should be rooted in sand mixed with peat moss.

Many tropicals must be rooted in an atmosphere high in humidity. This requirement is easily met by enclosing the cutting, with the rooting container, in a transparent plastic bag. The bag should be without holes and tightly closed. Quite often the cuttings, which have to be rooted under cover, also require bottom heat. To these applies the same as to the seeds, as already mentioned. Cuttings rooted under the cover do not need any additional water, escape of which is prevented by the enclosure. Even if some water evaporates, it condenses on the plastic cover and runs back. An open container, however, must be watered regularly, otherwise the rooting process will be interrupted by dryness.

Leaf Cutting

The most amazing rooting process is the raising of new plants from the cuttings of the leaves. This unique ability is reserved to a limited number of plants. Rex *Begonias,* some *Gesneriads, Peperomias,* and *Kalanchoes* are the best examples.

These plants have the ability to grow roots from any severed vein of the leaf. A healthy, not dying, leaf can produce many plants in this manner. Since people have been multiplying plants in this way, the question has often been asked, if that will happen also in nature. It does happen. The British botanist B. L. Burtt, who was studying *Gesneriads,* found in Borneo some leaves of a *Cyrtandra,* of the family *Gesnerias;* broken off and torn by winds, the leaves were rooting on the moist clay. What nature had endowed in plants is not limited in the wild, even if it is performed daily in front of our eyes.

In leaf-cutting propagation, the healthy leaf is cut into pie-shaped wedges. A strong vein should run roughly through its center, from the pointed end up. The wedge-shaped sections are not necessary; they just facilitate the rooting. Any section of leaf having a strong vein severed will do. The sections are inserted at an angle into the rooting medium, preferably sphagnum moss or some sterile, very moist mix. With a pencil, or a piece of sharpened wood, separate the medium to a depth of about a quarter inch, insert the section of leaf in such a way that the severed vein is in the bottom, and slightly press the rooting medium against the leaf section. Spacing is not very important — one inch is sufficient. The container with the leaf sections should be put into a tightly closed, transparent bag and set in a warm area as required for the germination of seeds.

Not all leaf cuttings are rooted under the cover. *Peperomias* and *Kalanchoes* root well without cover in the garden room, despite the lower night temperature. Rex *Begonias* and African violets require high humidity under the cover and continuous warm temperature.

Leaf-cutting propagation differs from the soft-hard-cuttings propagation in one important step: soft-hard cuttings grow roots and the cutting itself continues to grow, even blooms during the rooting process. On the contrary, the leaf cutting disintegrates after a new plant grows from the severed vein. In this respect, leaf-cutting propagation is approaching the raising of the plants from seeds.

Stem Cuttings

Many members of the arum and lily family exhibit another propagation peculiarity.The thick stem sections can be cut into sections about three inches long, each having at least one "eye" (raised portion). The open cuts on ends should be dusted with sulphur to prevent rot. Sections are then set into sand lengthwise, half buried. Roots will grow into the moist sand and a new plant will sprout from the "eye." After new shoots grow to the height of several inches, the new plant can be carefully lifted with its roots, and planted directly in a pot. The stem section should again be half buried into the soil as it was previously in the sand.

Some of the plants that can be propagated in this manner are: *Aglaonema, Dieffenbachia, Philodendron, Dracaena, Cordyline terminalis.*

Runners and Offshoots

Plants like *Episcia* send out long runners. When a runner reaches the soil in a lower pot, it roots there. The rooted shoot can be cut off from the mother plant, lifted with its roots, and planted as a new plant. Long runners can be cut into sections several inches long, each with a few leaves, and rooted in sand.

Chlorophytum (spider plant) sends ready-made plants on a long string. Such a rosette can be simply cut off and potted.

Some *Bromeliads,* members of the arum and palm family, also produce ready-made plants in the form of the offshoots. When of sufficient size, offshoots can be easily separated from the mother plant and put in their own pots.

Air Layering (Mossing)

Many people owning a large rubber plant and wanting to propagate it from the cuttings are disappointed. The *Ficus* (rubber plant) is most suitably propagated by air layering.

A section of a branch, selected for a new plant, is split lengthwise with a sharp knife. To keep the split open, a piece of toothpick or a small stone is inserted between the two halves. Then a ball of moist sphagnum moss is wrapped around the split and protected from outside with a wrap of plastic. The plastic wrap confines the humidity. From the incision roots will grow into the moss. When roots are of sufficient size, the new plant is cut off below the moss ball and transplanted.

17
The Insect Enemies

Insects are the plants greatest benefactors and its greatest enemies. Without the friendly insect accomplishing the pollination, the propagation of many plants would be doomed. Other friendly insects take care of the insect pest and keep plants healthy. In any balanced eco-system, mutual dependence works to mutual benefit.

An indoor garden, created by man, represents an unbalanced eco-system, depending on man for its balance. The wanted pollination and all the insect control becomes then the task of man.

It is ironic that plants in an indoor garden have to be defended against the insect, which is barely visible to the naked eye. Only such tiny insects can penetrate the fairly tight enclosure of an indoor garden. Insects of this type are not chewing but sucking and their presence is discovered generally after their destructive work is well advanced.

Since the insect endangering the plants in the garden room is so tiny, it is worthwhile to keep a magnifying glass on hand. It should magnify at least three times. I use one with eight-times magnification, which is very useful. Not all brown spots are caused by insects, neither are white spots. Whenever something like that is discovered on leaves, only a good magnifying glass will tell if it is the insect at work, or if a white spot is a deposit from an evaporated drop of water, or the pollen from another plant's blossom.

The resistance of plants to the insect varies greatly. Generally, the more a certain plant is cultivated and hybridized, the lower the resistance. The pineapple *(ananas)* belongs to the bromeliad family. *Bromeliads* are known to be attacked by scale only. However, pineapple, cultivated for at least 1,000 years, is infested, besides the scales, also by mealy bugs and spider mites. Compared to the other plants, it has an admirable record. Many plants cultivated for centuries have long catalogs of pests and diseases plaguing them. The rose leads with 17 diseases and 19 different pests, followed closely by *Chrysanthemum, Orchids, Iris, Dahlias,* and *Tulips*. Similarly, cultivated fruit is subjected to a long line of diseases and pests, with the apple leading and even surpassing the rose in numbers of possible enemies.

The first summer we had our garden room I received one day a telephone call from my wife: "Our roses in the garden room are sick." I was quite surprised. "No insect can get into the garden room," was my argument. Yet the leaves had yellow and light green spots, and some were falling off. The investigation with magnifying glass revealed active, eight-legged spider mites and tiny drops of their eggs. Several applications of rose dust seemed to bring them under control. But after a few weeks the damage was even greater. Not only were some branches of the rose trees defoliated, but many *Impatiens* were infested also. The long and hard fight with spider mites started.

After some spraying with Malathion, I discovered little progress. I had to learn the spider mites become immune to the insecticide and go around their usual business, only stopping to wait for the drenching spray of the sprayer to quit. I had to alternate the various insecticides after two or three sprayings. So it went from Malathion to Isotox, then Dimite, and finally Kelthane. That stopped the infestation. The trouble was, I stopped spraying too. Only later I had to make the decision to spray every week, in order to check the insects in the garden room.

The spider mites are the hardest insects to control. Under the heading of spider mites can be included also the cyclamen mite and clover mites. The name *red spider* is a collective name often used for any spider mite. All are related not only in appearance but also in their work, resistance, and the susceptibility to attack. Their eggs are not destroyed by insecticides and hatch into adults in a few days. This shows the necessity of weekly spraying. The admirable ability to develop immunity to all insecticides in a very short time makes it necessary to change sprays, at maximum, every third spraying. It is frustrating to watch them run merrily around shortly after drenching them with Malathion, Kelthane, or even alcohol, when they develop immunity to that particular poison.

Next on the list of difficult insects is the white fly. Tiny, white insects start to fly around when you touch a plant on which they are feeding. The ability to fly makes them hard to pursue, but the white color gives them away. The faithful weekly spraying with Malathion, Isotox, or Pyrethrin will eventually eradicate them. It will take several weeks, but if sprayed weekly, the white fly does not have a chance.

When you discover small, white, fluffy balls on leaves, stems, or leaf axis, that means another trouble: mealy bugs. The white, fluffy ball is a waxy, protective coating, resisting almost all insecticides. Only a good spray of Malathion or an application of alcohol can penetrate it. Alcohol is applied with a small cotton ball on a toothpick or stick; in touching the waxy coating, the alcohol will dissolve it immediately, and a light brown colored bug will be seen. It is a female, hatching the young ones. The male and the young are very small, without the white, waxy protection, and are easily destroyed by any general-purpose insecticide. Their presence is discovered by black, sooty patches left behind on the leaves. Mealy bugs move around slowly and are not particular about their food. Almost any plant can be attacked.

Fairly easily eradicated are aphids. The tiny green or brown insect can be seen in swarms feasting on the young shoots of plants. Several sprays of Pyrethrin, Malathion, or Isotox can remove them completely.

Spider mites, white fly, mealy bugs, and aphids are the most common insects in a garden room. But it is also possible to get some others, like thrips, scale, slugs, and nematodes. Thrips are similar to mites and the treatment is the same. Scale form small deposits of hard shells under which they hide. The best is to scrape them off and then to spray with Malathion. Slugs, the small, slimy, snaillike creatures, sometimes enter the garden room. They feed mostly at night on leaves, chewing up whole sections. During the day they hide in dark places. Besides the vegetative diet, slugs are fond of beer, which is the eradicator of slugs. Beer, put in a shallow pan will attract slugs; they go for a drink—and drown. Beer is about five times more effective than methaldehyde bait, which is more tedious to prepare and more difficult to remove dead slugs from. If beer is used, the drowned slugs are simply thrown out with the beer.

The insect springtail, when discovered in the soil or on top, is the easiest to get rid of. The tobacco from a cigarette is spread on top of the soil of a pot and the plant watered. Nicotine, leached out from the tobacco, will kill the springtails swarming on or in the soil. An application of Malathion will do the same job.

In contrast to all the insects to be discovered on plants, nematodes live in the soil. Tiny, microscopic organisms, they penetrate into the roots, and slowly choke off any plant. Nematodes are known to attack about 2,000 different plants. When a plant is stunned, does not grow, looks sick, and otherwise is free from insects, nematodes can be suspected. The plant should be then lifted from the pot, and soil removed from the roots. The presence of nematodes can be seen in the swollen root, having numerous bumps, balls, or thick rings around them. (The distinction should be made, however, between some plants producing bulbils on roots, by which it can be propagated, like *Asparagus, Chlorophytum, Ceropegia, Alocasia,* etc.).

Cuttings can be taken from a plant stunned by nematodes. The rest, especially the roots, has to be burned and soil thrown away or burned also.

Nematodes get into the garden room with the soil. The best protection is to use nematode-free soil. In climates with winter freeze of several feet in depth, nematodes are not a problem, since the freezing temperature destroys them. Any humusy soil (black dirt) can be safely used without sterilization. Where freezing is mild, sterilized soil should be used.

It is also possible to treat soil with a product called VC-13, which kills nematodes. VC-13 has an offensive smell present for several days after the treatment, which can be done outside or in a garage. Treated soil can be used immediately for potting, or after the evaporation of the offensive smell. VC-13 is a very safe nemacide and fast acting. Nemagon and Fumagon are also safe, but very slow acting. Other nemacides on the market are quite dangerous to handle and require a period of 2 to 3 weeks before the treated soil can be used for potting.

Soil treated with VC-13 is only partly sterilized. The insects in the soil are killed; however, the seeds of weeds are untouched.

Besides being attacked by insects, plants suffer from diseases. Leaf spot, blight, and stem rot are caused by bacteria. Fungi cause mildew, rust, scab, and leaf galls. Many fungi can be controlled by proper environmental conditions. Humidity over eighty percent without any air circulation supports the growth of mildew and leaf spot.

Plants can be protected from fungi by the use of the proper fungicide. The old therapy is the well-known garden sulphur in the form of fine powder. Another old standby is Bordeaux mixture, used to control leaf spot and blight. New excellent fungicides are Captan and Zineb, which are the best and safest of many fungicides now available. Besides being used for the same purpose as sulphur, Captan and Zineb also control crown rot and root rot.

All fungicides now available are only protective types. They do not eradicate the disease.

18
Insecticides–The Weapon

The tolerance of the insect and its reaction to certain poisons is admirable. Plant juices that are harmless to many insects will kill man or animal. Other substances harmless to man will easily kill the same insect.

Some insects live in plants that concentrate the metal selenium from the soil. If sheep or cattle eat such plants, they die within several hours from selenium poisoning. All parts of oleander *(Nerium)* are very poisonous to man in minute quantities. Cutting a stick from a branch of oleander to roast a hot dog on a picnic in Florida, will kill any person. Yet mealy bugs will happily feast on leaves of the oleander. Its juices, which kill man, do not harm mealy bugs. However, alcohol concentration of 30 percent will instantly kill any mealy bug, although much higher concentrations are harmless to man. Similarly, aphids can feast on oleander with impunity, but are instantly killed with 0.02 percent concentration of *Pyrethrum,* which is harmless to people and animals.

Much emphasis has recently been put on the harmfulness of insecticides. It is perhaps of some value, where animals might get hurt by indiscriminate use. However, in the enclosed garden there is no such danger. The only danger from spraying of insecticides is the inhaling of spray by the person doing the spraying. Fortunately we have a very safe insecticide: pyrethrin.

Pyrethrin

Pyrethrin is extracted from a daisylike flower: *Chrysanthemum cinerariaefolium.* It can be grown any place, but commercially it is mostly grown in Africa and in Ecuador. Actually, it is one of the oldest insecticides, being discovered accidentally by a housewife in Yugoslavia. When she threw out some wilted daisies, next day she found cockroaches lying dead around the wilted flowers. That was the beginning of Pyrethrin as an insecticide.

Pyrethrin is the safest insecticide, killing insects on contact, without leaving a residue. Any time an insecticide is labeled safe to people and animals, it is Pyrethrin. Its recent massive use was spearheaded by the war in Southeast Asia, where it proved to be an excellent protection from insects. An aerosol can of Pyrethrin belonged to the equipment of a soldier.

To make Pyrethrin a general purpose insecticide, rotenone is added. Rotenone, or cube, is extracted from the roots of some tropical trees like *Derris.*

The combination *Pyrethrin*-rotenone is sold either as a concentrate to be mixed with water, or in aerosol cans for quick action. The aerosol can is very effective, if instructions are followed and the plant is sprayed from a distance of 24 inches or more. Spraying from a closer range will damage the foliage or even the stems. The propellant in the can is a refrigerant—the same that is used to freeze food in a freezer. I made some tests, spraying the contents of an aerosol can of insecticide on an open bulb thermometer. The thermometer showed initially, in all cases, 69° F. When I sprayed from a distance of 24 inches for five seconds, the temperature dropped to 52° F. Under the same conditions, spraying from a distance of 18 inches, the thermometer showed 45° F. Spraying from 6 inches, the temperature was 39° F. Such a sudden drop of 17°–30° F within a few seconds is detrimental to any soft tropical plant. Normally, in their habitat or in our homes, they never experience such a plunge of temperature. The reaction, then, is dropping of leaves, parts of leaves frozen, or dying of stems or even of the whole plant.

Pyrethrin is effective against all plant pests — except mealy bugs. It has to be alternated with Malathion at least every 3 to 4 weeks. This is not only to check and prevent the spreading of mealy bugs, but to interrupt the continuity of spray which might make spider mites immune.

Malathion

Malathion is almost indispensable — until some equivalently effective insecticide is found. It is nearly a universal insect killer. Despite its offensive smell, you cannot afford *not* to use it. The importance of malathion is in its ability to destroy mealy bugs. And you never know where these pests will show up.

Once I was confident that I had all the insects in the garden room under control. For 10 weeks I used nothing but "Red Arrow," which is a Pyrethrin, for weekly spraying. No insects were visible. Then one day I discovered mealy bugs on seven plants. Seven plants attacked from 350 is a very small percentage, but a disturbing one, since mealy bugs are persistent pests. Immediately I sprayed with Malathion and continued for four weeks. Then I returned to "Red Arrow," but every third spraying was with Malathion to prevent mealy bugs from taking hold.

Not all plants can take Malathion. It is not recommended on *Kalanchoe, Lantanas, Crassulas,* and some ferns. Heavy spray will kill *Anthurium* and defoliate *Fittonias. Fittonias,* however will recover after some time and grow new leaves. Blossoms of African violets will turn brown and then die. Dipping cuttings from infested *Euonymus japonicus, Coleus,* and *Impatiens* in a solution of Malathion will kill the more tender ones. Malathion is ineffective against spittlebugs, which attack *Chrysanthemum* and Roses. The spittlebug protects himself with a ball of foam. It can be controlled by spraying with Methoxychlor or Isotox. These pests are seldom found in an indoor garden, occuring more outdoors.

Premium-grade Malathion is called Cythion. It has a lower odor content than the regular grade.

Isotox

Isotox is another general-purpose insecticide, effective against many plant pests—except the mealy bugs.

Dimite and Kelthane are special sprays effective against spider mites only. The collective name, miticides, indicates that they are used for killing mites. Unless used exclusively against mites, it is good to combine them with Isotox, to achieve the control of other insects with one spraying. The main disadvantage of Isotox is its offensive smell, lingering in the air for days.

Systemics

A different group of insecticides is the type called *systemic*. It is applied to the soil either as granules or dissolved in water. Granules dissolve slowly and release the poison, which is absorbed by the system of the plant. In effect, the whole plant is being poisoned. Any sucking insect, such as aphids, mites, or mealy bugs, are poisoned with the nourishment they take from the plant. The effects of systemics last from 6 weeks to 4 months. The first systemic was sodium selenate, a violent poison, now outlawed. Presently only Systox is used. This treatment is not for every plant. Some will succumb very easy. Roses, *Impatiens,* and many *Gesneriads* appear to be most tolerant.

Shell Strip

One insecticide is the Shell Vapona strip, which is very easy to use: just hang it. The Shell strip is a solid stick, slowly giving out insect-killing gas. However, prolonged breathing of this gas is dangerous also to people. Since the garden room is connected to the house, it is not advisable to use it there because people will be present. In an indoor garden it can be used overnight, with all ventilation openings closed. Next morning, the indoor garden and adjacent room must be well ventilated.

The Shell strip is effective about four months. When not in use and tightly wrapped in plastic, its effectiveness is longer. The most effective use of Shell strip is in the quarantine of individual, infested plants. For such, treatment is needed a plastic bag, large enough for complete enclosure of the plant, and a section of Shell strip. The strip is hung on a stick or directly on the plant. The plastic bag is tightly closed for 2 to 4 hours. Within that time all insects are killed. Longer treatment is harmful to plants and when left so overnight, plants will succumb.

The majority of insecticides are available in two forms: wettable powder and emulsifiable concentrate. The concentrate is liquid and preferably used. When using powder dissolved in water, on some broad-leaf plants, spots of the powder are left after the water evaporates. Such spots are hard to remove.

Insecticides mixed for use cannot be stored for the next spraying. They become weak and ineffective. It is better to dispose of the leftover mix than to be fooled into effective spraying by using an ineffective mix. In using the insecticides, it is not the one teaspoon that counts. It is the effort of spraying and ventilating the room that should be taken into account.

Heavy drenching with insecticides can kill some plants and damage others. *Impatiens* are quite sensitive, and I lost several to heavy spraying. Tender new shoots of roses can be damaged or burned with heavy drenching. If fighting an infestation, it is better to apply a fog of insecticide, not damaging, and to apply it every 3 to 4 days. Spraying at intervals of several days is necessary to get rid of insects. At least three sprayings are required. Normally, an insecticide does not destroy the eggs already on the plants, only adults.

Some insecticides are dangerous. Chlordane, Cygon, and Lindane can be absorbed directly by the skin and therefore it is advisable to wear protective clothing. Better yet, do not use these when a good selection of safe insecticides is available.

All insecticides have to be administered with a sprayer. An array of sprayers is on the market. I tried several and finally keep using the Hudson's Constant Spray. It is a hand pump with a brass adjustable nozzle and a brass dip tube, removable for cleaning. The brass parts are very important, since all insecticides and their vehicles are corrosive. The Constant Spray feature makes it possible to pump more air into the reservoir and the sprayer continues to distribute the spray, fed by the compressed air. This is very handy. It frees one hand to bend a plant or to go with the sprayer down to the floor, in order to direct the stream of fog on the underside of the leaves. When the adjustable nozzle is turned to coarse spray, it shoots out a heavy fog of insecticide, which can rise from below and deposit on the underside of leaves, where most insects like to hide.

Constant Spray costs more than a simple sprayer. However, it lasts longer and performs better. After each use the sprayer should be flushed twice with clear water, which should also be forced through the nozzle, the excess water drained and shaked out and the cap left off, to facilitate drying of the tank.

Also available are mechanical sprayers and paint sprayers powered by electricity. Their usage is a little easier since it is not necessary to pump the air by hand. However, cleaning is messier. After each use they have to be flushed with kerosene to prevent rusting, and the moving parts are quite touchy. I stopped using them.

No perfect insecticide is available. Although several good ones are on the market, all put the user through the suffering of the offensive smell. The next improvement should be an insecticide without the foul odor.

19

Insect-free Plants

The dream of the millions is to have insect-free plants! Not only farmers, but horticulturists and plant lovers have such a wish. Even every primitive, trying to raise some crops with simple tools has the same idea.

It remains only a dream! The plants are destined to be the food of the world — not only the food of people and animals, but of insects as well.

If every rule has its exception, then the subjugation of plants to insects has some, too. There are insect-free plants—only a few, but they are available. Some are completely free, others are attacked by only one kind of insect. By selecting exclusively such plants for an indoor garden, it is possible to live with plants without the need of spraying for insects. And the blossoms can be enjoyed also.

The resistance of plants to insects varies greatly. We are tempted to assume that *Ginko biloba,* ferns, *Cycas,* and *Sequoia* (redwood), which all survived from the age of the dinosaurs, will be disease and insect resistant. This is true only about the maidenhair tree *(Ginko biloba)*. Ferns are subjected to a number of diseases and are attacked by aphids, scales, mealy bugs, cutworms, weevil, white fly, and snail. *Cycas* have enemies in scale, mealy bugs, thrips, and a blight, which causes death of the entire plant. *Sequoias* are endangered in a similar way to *Cycas*. On the other hand, *Aspidistra elatior,* called Cast-Iron Plant, is not so iron clad, since it can be infested by scale.

Some insect-free plants are known to people, as indicated by the name: bugbane *(Cimicifuga)*. Insect-free plants can be found in our temperate zone and in the tropics. Their number is relatively small, but enough to provide any indoor garden with a variety of blossoms and foliage.

Any insect-free plant is subjected to some disease, mostly to leaf spot caused by bacteria, or powdery mildew, or blight caused by fungi. Nematodes spare few plants, but *that* problem can be solved by using sterilized soil or by treating it with a good nemacide such as VC -13. The insect-free plants are generally subjected to a lesser number of diseases than plants attacked by some insects. Also in this way are minimized problems caused by bacteria, fungus, and virus.

When insect-free plants are grown in an indoor garden, there is no danger that insects, which make their way into the enclosure, will attack the available plants if they cannot find the preferable food. It has been proven by experiments,* that insects will starve to death rather than feed on plants that are resistant to that particular pest. The insect-free plants are either poisonous to the insect or, as their food, have many deficiencies, which limit and hinder growth and propagation of the insect pest.

Insect-free plants
suitable for an indoor garden†

Abelias
Aglaonemas

*See pp. 70-73 of *Insect-Pest Management and Control.* Publication 1695, Washington D.C.: National Academy of Sciences, 1969.

†This list represents sixty-seven insect-free plants described in this book.

Aloysia triphylla (Lemon verbena)
Alternantheras
Aristolochias
Bischofia javanica
Bouvardias
Carica papaya
Chlorophytums (Spider plant)
Cobea scandens (Cup-and-saucer vine)
Colocasias (Elephant ear)
Convolvulus (Dwarf morning glory)
Cryptomeria japonica (Dwarf Japanese cedar)
Cupheas (Cigar Flower)
Eranthemum nervosum
Eucharis grandiflora (Amazon lily)
Felicias
Iresine
Leucothoe catesbaei (Sweet bells)
Nandina domestica (Heavenly bamboo)
Oxalis
Peperomias
Philodendrons
Sansevierias
Scindapsus

Plants attacked by one insect *

Plant	*Insect*
Aloe	*Scale*
Alamandas	*White fly*
Ardisia crispa	*Scale*
Aspidistra elatior	*Scale*
Aucuba japonica	*Scale*
Bougainvilleas	*Scale*
Bromeliad family (all except pineapple)	*Scale*
Carissa grandiflora	*Thrips*
Kalanchoes	*Scale*
Osmanthus	*Scale*
Podocarpus	*Scale*
Scilla violacea	*Narcissus white fly*
Syngoniums	*Thrips*

The first group is an all-time choice. Not only does it do away with insecticides and bug hunting but it also provides an indoor garden with all necessary requirements. Fragrance is furnished by flowers of *Abelia, Bouvardia,* and *Eucharis.* Blossoms are supplied by *Aristolochia, Cobea, Cuphea, Eranthemum nervosum,* and *Oxalis.* Color is provided by *Aglaonema, Alternanthera, Iresine,* and *Peperomia.* The balance of plants offers good foliage on low plants or large leaves on shrubs of different height.

The other group, formed by plants attacked by one insect pest, will also provide fragrance, color, and variegated foliage. In introducing this group of plants, care should be taken not to bring in some insect. Every plant should be put for 2 to 4 hours in a bag with Shell insect strip, to get rid of all unwanted invaders. In this manner, an insect-free Room of Delight can be expected.*

*This list represents forty-five plants, attacked by one insect, described in this book.

*Insect-free plants are often refered to as *insect-resistant plants.* Several universities and research stations are engaged in development of a number of insect-resistant agricultural plants.

The list of insect-free plants and the list of plants attacked by one insect is extrapolated from the book by Pascal P. Pirone, *Diseases and Pests of Ornamental Plants,* Fourth Edition. Copyright © 1970 The Ronald Press Company, New York. Used with permission.

20
Three Plant Families

The backbone of the plants of indoor gardens are three plant families: *Begonias, Bromeliads,* and *Gesneriads*. Each comprises several thousand members and each alone can furnish plants and flowers for any season. A short introduction is presented here and the suitable plants are described in different sections, according to the characteristics each plant offers: suitable either for light transmitting or solid roof, be it everblooming, colorful foliage plant, special effect plant, or plain foliage plant.

Begonias

The gorgeous blossoms of tuberous *Begonia* capture everybody's eyes. These, together with wax *Begonias,* are the most popular. Unfortunately, hundreds of other begonias are little known. The begonia family is a large one and its members can be found in all tropical regions of the world. This explains the diversity of habits and variety of forms: from a very small *B.* 'Baby Rainbow' to the gigantic *B. coccinea,* with canes more than two inches thick, reaching to the height of twenty-five feet. The uninteresting green leaves of some wax *Begonias* are in contrast with the color variations of rhizomatous and especially with the gay coloring of *Begonia rex.* Not even the leaf forms can be called typical. The starlike shape of *B. kenworthyi* is very different from the typical angel-wing *Begonia,* and differs even more from *B. luxurians,* which looks like a palm.

Begonias are divided according to their rootstock: tuberous, rhizomatous, and fibrous rooted. Tuberous are not adaptable to the garden room since they require a cool and dry atmosphere; it is, however, advantageous to start these in an indoor garden before setting them outdoors. Rhizomatous are undemanding plants with thick rhizomes crawling on or above soil and beautiful foliage. Fibrous rooted are all other *Begonias* not fitting into the previous two groups. Most notable are the cane-type plants, also called "angel wing," producing numerous cane shoots from the base and large clusters of blossoms, very easy to grow and blooming often. Not so easy to cultivate are complicated hybrids of rex *Begonias,* demanding more attention but highly rewarding with beautifully colored leaves.

This division is very approximate; in the fibrous-rooted group are so many different *Begonias* that do not even behave like cousins. Take for example *B. semperflorens,* the common wax *Begonia.* Robust and rugged, it can grow in sun or shade, blooms constantly, and requires dry soil. In direct contrast, the kingly *Begonia rex* would be surely killed by direct sun, dry soil, and dry air.

Coming from so many different regions of the world, *Begonias* have very different cultural requirements. Between the extremes of the just-mentioned *B. semperflorens* and *B. rex,* the great majority want filtered light, humid air, and moist soil. Most *Begonias* will bloom only when they have light coming from above.

Many contradictions are unexplained in the behavior of members of this family. The wax *Begonia,* which will rot in soil moist for a prolonged period of time, will happily start roots on a cutting in a glass of water, even bloom there. The finicky rex, so afraid of dry air, cold drafts, and sun, will generate a host of plantlets from a leaf severed away from the plant, cut in small sections and simply laid on moist soil. Most *Begonias* are long-lived plants: 15 and more years is not unusual. All start from dustlike seed, be it the miniature or the giant.

This family alone furnished all necessary colors and flowers all year, not only the *Semperflorens*; but also few angel wings blooming always, and others that bloom several times a year, and still others that bloom only once. Many *Begonias* bloom in summer. In winter the rhizomatous start blooming in December and continue well into the spring. White and pink are their specialty. When out of bloom, their variegated foliage contributes color: silver on green, pink and silver, black margins, pink ruffles, maroon leaves, red underside — all to break the green monotony.

Begonias were named in honor of Michel Begon, the French governor of Santo Domingo (the island of Hispanola), on whose expedition into the interior of the island the first *Begonias* were found in 1690.

Bromeliads

One of the most delicious fruits we know—the pineapple— belongs to the *Bromeliad* family. The long and narrow leaves, forming a rosette, found on a fresh pineapple, are representative of almost all *Bromeliads*.

The *ananas*—pineapple—grows in the soil. This, however, is not the most common habitat of the family. Some grow in soil, rocks, and sand, behaving and looking like a desert cactus. The great majority of *Bromeliads* grow in trees not to suck the juices, just to perch there. With wirelike legs they clamp firmly to the trunk or branch and derive all their food from the air. For this purpose they are especially equipped. The leaves of many *Bromeliads* form a container or cup in the center of the rosette, in which the rainwater and dew collect and are held. Large specimens in tropical forests can hold up to one or two gallons of water in this manner. Those little pools of water high in the trees are not lifeless. Algae, moss, frogs, and snakes make their home in the leaf-cups of *Bromeliads* and provide them, in turn, with some fertilizer.

Tillandsias form a group of *Bromeliads* living high in the trees and do not have any means of holding the rainwater. The origin of the name *Tillandsia* is very interesting. In giving names to plants, Carolus Linneus, the originator of systematic botany, liked to use a play on words, practical jokes, and made-up names from actual events. Knowing that one of his students was afraid to sail on a ship and would rather travel several hundred miles on hard roads, he used the name *tillands — land rover —* in the opposite meaning: afraid of water. The name *Tillandsia* was then used by Linneus for the *Bromeliads* protected on their leaves by scales. Linneus thought the leaf scales protected *Tillandsias* from water and consequently the plants were afraid of water. Actually, the opposite is true: the leaf-scales on *Tillandsias* are moisure-gathering organs. The leaf-scales not only transmit the rainwater to the vital leaf organs but they also have the capability to absorb water vapor directly from the air. The best known *Tillandsia,* in this respect, is Spanish moss *(Tillandsia usneoides)*, which can live on telephone wires, without any contact with any living organism.

Bromeliads are confined to the Americas (only one was found in West Africa), and can then be called typical American plants. However they are not so much cultivated in the Americas as in Europe, where they have been appreciated as house plants for more than 150 years. Only after World War II *Bromeliads* became more known in United States through the efforts of Mulford B. Foster from Orlando, Florida. A plant lover and collector, he made several trips to Brazil, on which he found many new *Bromeliads,* and can claim the largest number ever discovered by an individual. Eighteen *Bromeliads* carry his name and two that of his wife, Racine. Also one genus, *Fosterella,* is named in his honor.

Since the pineapple family are typical American plants, they deserve to be more known and grown. *Bromeliads* are very grateful plants — undemanding, almost insect free, requiring minimum maintenance. The maintenance of *Bromeliads* is very easy. Plants having the center cup — like *Aechmea, Billbergia, Neoregelia, Nidularium* and *Vriesea* – must have water in the cup. If the water dries out, it only slows down the development of that particular plant. In fertilizing, only weak fertilizer is used once in six or eight weeks—for best results, applied to the soil in the pot, rather than to water in the cup. (If water dries out, the leftover of powdered fertilizer might damage the plant.) Free from insects, only scale bothers them.

The light conditions vary: plants with colorful markings require more light than plain green foliage. *Bromeliads* adapt easily to the low light and humidity levels found in our houses. A great boon is the summer spent outside under the trees.

Each *Bromeliad* blooms only once in its lifetime. (Few exceptions to this are not suitable for indoor culture.) After flowering the plant does not die right away. First it sends out side shoots, which can be broken off when sufficiently long and hard at the base, and potted. Side shoots left on the mother plant will develop into mature specimens, still connected to the original plant. Normally 2 to 3 shoots will grow after flowering, with exception of *Cryptanthus,* which keeps producing offshoots for each one cut off, up to 18 from one plant. Some *Vrieseas* produce only one shoot in the center. Not all *Bromeliads* will produce offshoots after flowering. Many species of *Vriesea* and *Tillandsia* are lacking such capability and must be propagated from seed only.

The mature *Bromeliads* can be forced into bloom by small quantities of ethylene gas. Apples give off this gas in just the right concentration. To hasten blooming time of *Bromeliads,* the cup has to be first emptied of water (if it is a plant having a leaf cup). The plant is then put into a plastic bag with one or two apples and the bag is closed air tight. After five days of exposure to the ethylene gas, the *Bromeliad* is removed from the bag and the cup filled with water. Flowering should start in 4 to 6 weeks.

The tree-perching *Bromeliads* can be grown in a pot or attached to a dry branch, driftwood, or bark. The plant should be first tied with a wire, preferably plastic insulated electrical wire, never galvanized or copper wire. Later it will develop its own wiry legs and live so happily without any attention. If it is a *Tillandsia* it won't even need watering. Other plants will require filling the cup with water. Any tree-dwelling *Bromeliad* can also be grown in soil, where the wiry legs will develop into small roots for collecting nourishment and holding the plant upright.

Bromeliads vary much in size. Some *Neoregelias* and *Tillandsias* do not grow larger than two or three inches and are suitable for terrariums. The *Puyas,* from the Andes mountains in Peru, are real giants, having trunks 13 feet high with three-feet-long leaves. At flowering time, the inflorescence shoots up another 17 feet high like a tall candle. Such a flowering tower exhausts the plant, which dies after scattering seeds.

Many *Bromeliads* offer nice color selection: red, pink, purple, golden-yellow, or silver are alternated with plants having stripes and crossband markings. Some change the already colorful foliage to vivid red in the center at flowering time.

Gesneriads

Gesneriad is a huge family of plants! Its members are found mostly in tropical regions of the Americas, Asia, and Africa. Even in Europe some *Gesneriads* grow, which are not tropical but alpine plants, growing high in the mountains of the Balkans and the Pyrenees.

Gesneriads in cultivation are from the tropics. It is interesting that one of the last-discovered plants of this family became the most known one of all *Gesneriads:* the *Saintpaulia* — African violet — which has become the No. 1 American house plant. Its constant bloom and adaptability to house conditions puts it in first place among house plants.

However, few *Gesneriads* are good house plants, besides the African violet. Mostly, they require higher humidity for proper flowering than is available in the house. In a garden room, *Aeschynanthus* and *Columneas* can fill hanging baskets or cascade down from a shelf. The *Episcias,* with brightly colored leaves, can be put in any warm corner having filtered light. *Sinningia speciosa,* better known as florist *Gloxinia,* will brighten any spot with its large trumpet flowers — that is, when in active growth and out of dormancy.

Anthurium andraeanum

Gesneria cuneifolia

Cuphea platycentra

Episcia cupreata 'Chocolate soldier'

Besides *Gloxinia,* many other *Gesneriads* require rest and go dormant: *Rechsteineria,* growing also from a tuber; plants with scaly rhizomes like *Achimenes, Kohleria,* real *Gloxinia,* and *Smithianta.* These require attention when they wake up from dormancy, in a darker and cooler place, where they have to be put again after the active and flowering period.

Streptocarpus (Cape primrose) is an easy plant, bringing a variety of colors to the house or an indoor garden during its long flowering period. A little-known plant, with qualities of the African violet, is *Gesneria cuneifolia,* an everblooming plant from a tribe that gave the name to the whole family.

Many other *Gesneriads* are cultivated by specialists and fanciers. These plants are generally available from seed funds of *Gesneriad* societies. Some nurseries specialize in *Gesneriads* only and handle the less popular plants.

Gesneriads were named after Conrad Gesner, the sixteenth-century naturalist.

21

Watering Key

MOIST: Keep soil moist all the time. Such plants can even stand in a bowl of water and will do admirably on wick watering.

MODERATELY MOIST: Water when the top of soil is dry.

MODERATELY DRY: Allow to dry between waterings.

DRY: In the hot summer, water twice a week, otherwise once a week. Exception are spiny cacti, not to be watered more often than once a month, sparingly.

Some plants will not bloom if all of the soil is not continually moist, including the bottom of pot. In watering, the water must always be added until it starts to leak out below the pot. The water collected in the saucer should be poured away. This type of watering is necessary for: *Acalypha* 'Ceylon,' *Anthurium andreanum, Clerodendrum thomsonae, Crossandra infundibuliformis, Dipladenia sanderi, Episcias, Gesneria cuneifolia, Ixoras, Manettia inflata, Medinilla magnifica.*

22
The Everblooming Plants

The everblooming plants are the best return for our investment, gratefully paying back, day after day. The continuous supply of blossoms is the reward for our care.

Like all beauties, the everblooming plants are a problem, also. The blossoms of loveliness are not permanent. When spent, they have to be removed. The clean-up is then our pay for the performance of colors and forms. Just like in a family: the childless couple has less cleaning — but misses smiles, lively chatter, and the beauty that children bring.

Everblooming Plants
for
Light-transmitting Roof Structures

Allophyton Mexicanum
Mexican Foxglove

The Mexican Foxglove is a small rosette of wedge-shaped leaves, above which rise stalks carrying flowers of lavender color. Its blossoms are only a half-inch long, coming in quick succession. To support the continuous bloom, the Mexican foxglove has to be kept moist. It is a thirsty plant. It is a proven house plant in good light next to the window. Propagation is by seeds or by division of older plants.

Begonia 'Corallina De Lucerna'

This is a hybrid named after Lake Lucerne in Switzerland. It has large, dark green, silver-spotted leaves of satin sheen and huge, pendulous clusters of coral pink flowers (up to 50 in a single cluster). It often blooms as a cutting in water. It grows easily to five feet in height in a few years. When a cane shoots up high without flowering, cut it off at midpoint. Soon it will develop a new branch and blossom. It is good also as a house plant, but it will not flower under a solid roof without light above. The underside of the leaves is deep red. Keep it moderately moist. *Corallina* means *coral-red.*

Begonia Fuchsioides

A fibrous-rooted *Begonia* with small, dark-green, toothed leaves and arching branches. The red, drooping flowers look like flowers of *Fuchia,* hence the name *'fuchsioides.'* It needs warmth, high humidity, and an abundance of moisture (moderately moist soil).

Begonia 'President Carnot'

Cane type or Angel-Wing Begonia. A hybrid of *'Corallina de Lucerna'* and similar to it. Its large,

Allophyton mexicanum.

green leaves are sometimes silver-spotted, with a red underside, and it has large trusses of carmine-red blossoms. It needs less light than Corallina. Keep it moderately moist. It is named for a president of France.

Begonia 'Preussen'

This Fibrous-rooted *Begonia* has small, green leaves, silver spotted on the young plant, and large, pink flowers. For bushy growth it should be pinched. Keep it moderately moist. The name means *Prussia,* one of the former States of Germany.

Begonia Semperflorens

The well-known wax *Begonias* have a name that truly expresses their best ability: everblooming! The common name wax alludes to the glossy leaves, which are as abundant as the flowers. And what leaves they have! — small or large, in all shades of green, even bronze, sometimes edged with red. The profusion of flowers comes in a wide variety of colors and shapes: white, pink, red, yellow, single, double, or semi-double. Their vitality is to be admired also. Outside the house, in full sun or full shade, indoor with only light that a window lets in — this plant is always in bloom! When old and leggy, just prune them back severely and they come back with new vigor, eager for more bloom. It is easy to grow them, easy to keep them. Cuttings root in water and even bloom. But they insist on one requirement: no wet feet. Water only when they dry out. If the soil is kept moist and wet constantly they refuse to bloom — admirable plants! Some new hybrids, with double flowers, like miniature roses, do not branch easily. Tip cuttings, when rooted, grow into a single long shoot. In that case cuttings with several branches have to be rooted and several of them planted in one pot.

Begonia Semperflorens 'Charm'

One wax *Begonia* to be singled out for its unusually colored foliage. The leaves are marbled with cream and yellow so much that very little green is left. Flowers are single pink and complement the charming combination of colors. Of pendulous habit, it is nice in a basket or trailing down from a shelf. Keep it dry.

Beloperone Guttata
Shrimp Plant

The common name is derived from the unusual flowers, about 2 two inches long, hanging from the end of branches. The small white flowers are speckled maroon and partly hidden by overlapping, reddish-brown *bracts,* which give the appearance of the segments of a shrimp. The wiry branches carry small, somewhat hairy leaves. The shrimp plant, a native of Mexico, wants to be kept moderately dry, and wants bright light. Its winter flowering depends on the availability of light. When it becomes too straggly, cut down to four inches. This will encourage bushy new growth. Cuttings root in moist sand. The name *guttata* means *speckled.*

Browallia Speciosa

The number of plants providing blue blossoms for an indoor garden is rather limited. The deep-blue flowers of *Browallia* are a welcome contrast to the bright red, pink, and green of the garden room. This native to South America (Colombia) is a nice subject for a hanging basket or shelf. Its straggly habit is easily forgotten and the sight of one-inch flowers, which are larger than leaves. *Browallia* should be treated as an annual and cutting taken in time to provide replacement plants. Seeds germinate easily. Sun does not harm this plant and watering is needed often, daily in summer. The famous botanist Linneus named this plant for his friend Bishop Browall.

Capsicum Annuum Conoides
Christmas Pepper

The ornamental pepper, sold before Christmas for its red fruit, is treated as an annual. However, if supplied with continuous warmth and moisture, it will produce small, white flowers and red fruits all year. I keep one on the shelf above the heating radiation, and Christmas pepper loves it there. In this manner is simulated the climate of its native lands of the South American tropics, where the pepper grows as a perennial. Chill drafts will cause leaf drop.

After ripening, the conical fruit shrinks and the red color fades. That is the time for collecting fruit for seasoning and seeds. When opening the ripened fruits, touching the mouth or eyes will cause a burning sensation, which can be alleviated with good washing. Also, the hands have to be washed several times.

Red peppers belong to the potato family and not the black pepper family. Their requirement of moisture has to be always satisfied. Wick watering or standing in shallow pan of water is preferable. *Capsicum* means *small capsule; annuum: annual; conoides: like a cone.*

Columneas

Columneas are relatives of African violets and belong to the *Gesneriad* family. All originate exclusively in Central and South America, some in the Caribbean. They were named for the Italian botanist Columna. Most *Columneas* are trailing plants and make a beautiful display of foliage and flowers when grown in a hanging basket or on a shelf. The leaves are generally small, in many hues of green, on some plants *(Columnea gloriosa)* covered with reddish hair. That by itself is a sight! Yet it is the flowers of *Columnea* that make the real display. Mostly larger than leaves, up to three inches tall, they sit majestically erect on trailing vines. The slender tubular flower is topped with a wide, arching hood accented with two side lobes and a front lip. The color selection is worthy of the graceful form: two complementing colors of red and yellow, orange and red, gold and yellow — in different intensities and shades. Few *Columnea* species are everblooming, only *Columnea illepida, C. Zepidocaula* and *Columnea tulae 'Flava.'* Recent hybridizing brought a number of *Columneas* that are continually blooming. All are available from mail-order houses.

Everblooming *Columneas:*

C. Cornelian has narrow, dark-green leaves and smaller flowers, reddish brown and yellow. Some branches are upright, others drooping. A good house plant. *C.'Early Bird'* is a trailing plant with small leaves and large, orange-red and yellow flowers.

C. tulae 'Flava' has smallish leaves dwarfed by long, yellow flowers.

C.'Yellow dragon' Large leaves (for a Columnea), overpowered with bright, yellow flowers supplied in profusion.

When pollinated and developed, the seed pods of Columneas form white, soft balls, glistening among the foliage. Seeds are extracted from the ball by squashing on tissue paper and letting dry. Cuttings root easily in sand.

Crossandra Infundibuliformis

A shrub, which in India grows to the height of three feet, is satisfied in the pot to grow about eighteen inches tall. Above glossy, green leaves are always towering spikes bearing orange flowers. Before one spike is done flowering a new one is ready to supply more funnel-shaped blossoms. *Crossandra* starts blooming as a very small plant, is slow growing and not easily branching. Warmth, high humidity, and moist soil are essential for flowering. Cuttings root in sand, under transparent cover, and with bottom heat. *Infundi buliformis* means *funnelform.*

Crossandra infundibuliformis.

Dipladenia sanderi 'Rosea.'

Dipladenia Sanderi 'Rosea'

Dipladenias are woody vines native to tropical South America. They are sometimes also called *Mandevilla,* since both groups are very similar and belong to the same family. From many available in trade, only *Dipladenia sanderi 'Rosea'* is ever-blooming. The shiny green leaves are bronzy underneath. The flowers are larger than the leaves, up to three inches in diameter, rosy-pink with a pure yellow throat, shaped like a morning glory. It's not a vigorous climber, but starts blooming as a small plant. *Dipladenia* needs high humidity, filtered light, and continually moist soil. When watering, water must be added until it leaks from under the pot. The excess water, collected in a saucer, has to be poured away. If all of the soil ball is not kept moist, *Dipladenia* will not bloom. Cuttings need bottom heat for rooting. It is an excellent plant to have.

Euphorbia Splendens
Crown of Thorns

Although this plant is native to Madagascar and does not grow in Palestine, it is nevertheless associated with the Crucifixion. The long shoots of gray wood, with few leaves and full of spines, make it easy to imagine as material used for the crown of thorns for Jesus Christ.

Despite its somber appearance, *Euphorbia splendens* carries at the end of its branches clusters of rounded blossoms in salmon color, about a half inch in diameter. The grayish-green leaves fall off easily when the plant is grown too dry.

More desirable is *E. splendens bojeri,* also from Madagascar. It is called dwarf crown of thorns for its bushy and branching habit. Leaves are smaller, dark green, holding well on branches; grow in profusion, and hide the gray wood and spines. Clusters of rounded flowers are bright red.

Euphorbia splendens.

In good light or sun, Crown of Thorns will bloom all year. It has to be kept moderately dry. Cuttings root easily in moist sand. However, the milky sap, oozing from the cut, has to dry first for several hours before inserting the cutting into sand.

Splendens means *splendid.*

Euphorbia is named for Euphorbus, doctor of a king in Numidia in North Africa, who a few years before the coming of Jesus Christ, discovered medicinal properties of some members of this plant family.

Felicia
Blue Daisy; Blue Marguerite

This is a group of daisylike plants from South Africa. Some are annuals, others perennials, with mostly blue petals and large, yellow centers. All require bright light and can take full sun. Soil should be kept moist. It propagates easily from seeds or cuttings rooted in moist sand. It is named in honor of German official Felix.

F. amelloides is also called *Agathea coelestis* a perennial about 18 inches high. Single flowers grow on long stalks. *Amelloides* means *like amelus* (an Italian aster).

F. bergeriana is an annual. It is a small plant, reaching only 8 inches in height, and has blue flowers, smaller than in previous plants. Leaves are narrow like grass.

Felicia is an insect-free plant.

Fuchsia

F.'Rufus'
F. 'Swanley yellow'
See *Fuchsia* in section "Special-effect Plants."

Ervatamia Coronaria

Sometimes listed as *Tabernaemontana* and named so after a German botanist. It is a shrub from India, cultivated in the tropics for its glossy green leaves and white, fragrant flowers. Both leaves and flowers look much like *Gardenia,* although are not related to it. Its flowers are exquisite: pure white, waxy, undulating about one inch in diameter, growing in clusters. Many names were given to this unusual plant: Cape Jasmine, Butterfly Gardenia, East Indian Rose Bay. *Ervatamia* is slow growing; for continuous bloom it must have bright light, be kept moist, and fertilized often. *Coronaria* means *used for garlands.*

Impatiens

These well-known plants, used often in gardens, make excellent subjects for a garden room. Their ability to bloom constantly, without special care, is a great asset. The leaves are light or dark green, some variegated with cream, other with maroon blotches on the underside. Flowers come in a variety of colors: reds, pinks, orange, purple, white, double or single.

The everblooming *Impatiens* come to us from the island of Zanzibar, near the east coast of Africa, the land mysterious to the Arabs in past centuries. The branches of *Impatiens* are watery and brittle, but root very easily in water, where they often start to bloom and then continue blooming after transplanting.

A number of other *Impatiens* pride themselves with colorful foliage or large flowers; some are annuals, some perennials. The everblooming one, *Impatiens sultanii*, should be treated as an annual. If kept longer than a year and a half, it becomes straggly, losing lower leaves and flowering less; cuttings of old branches are hard to root.

Bright light, but not burning sun, and plenty of water are requirements for constant bloom.

Impatiens sultanii is well loved and known under many affectionate names: Patient Lucy, Busy Lizzie, Sultana, Touch-me-not. The name itself is an allusion to the impatience of ripened seed pods that burst on touch.

Jatropha

Two cultivars of *Jatropha pandurifolia,* which comes from the West Indies, are everblooming. The leaves have lobes, some look like three fingers or holly. Male and female flowers are separate, but on the same plant; although individual flowers are small, they are in clusters for greater effect. *Jatrophas* are grown outdoors in Southern Florida and are mainly obtainable from nurseries located there. Warmth, humidity, bright light, and moisture are their requirements.

Jatropha pandurifolia.

J. pandurifolia "Dwarf" is a plant of compact growing habit. With red flowers.

J. pandurifolia "Holly Leaf" has leaves resembling those of holly. Its flowers are orange-red.

The name *pandurifolia* means *fiddle-shaped leaves*.

Cuttings root easy in sand; the milky sap, dripping from the cut should first be allowed to dry.

Lantana Montevidensis
Trailing Lantana

Lantana is often seen outdoors in gardens or in planters. This is the summer blooming *Lantana camara*. The everblooming *Lantana montevidensis* is a trailing plant, a good subject for a hanging basket or dropping down from a shelf. It grows slowly; the wiry, woody branches carry small, rough leaves; when rubbed, the leaves give off a spicy, pleasant odor. The flowers are very small and form heads, an inch and a half in diameter, rosy-lavender in color, and slightly fragrant. A perennial, it requires bright light, even sunlight, and moderately moist soil. Cuttings of softwood root easily in sand. It is named for Montevideo, the capital of Uruguay. Avoid spraying with Malathion. Heavy spray will brown and shrink the blossoms.

Manettia Inflata (Bicolor)

The common name *firecraker plant* is an allusion to the fiery red and yellow colors of the flowers. *Manettia* is a climber with thin stems, small leaves, and one-inch long, tubular flowers, bright red with yellow tips. It is a ravenous grower filling the pot with roots easily, so much so that it pushes itself from the pot. It is best to grow it in a tub. Cuttings need bottom heat for rooting, to simulate

Manettia inflata.

the warm soil of tropical America, which is the home of *Manettia*. Filtered light and plenty of moisture are its requirements. It is named for an Italian botanist, Manetti. *Inflata* means *inflated; bicolor: two-colored.*

Oxalis Peduncularis

An everblooming *Oxalis* from Ecuador. Its pleasant green, wavy shamrock-like leaves on long stems are topped by clusters of orange-yellow flowers carried on long stalks. It needs bright light and wants to be kept dry. The name *Oxalis* means *sour* in allusion to its sour juice. *Peduncularis* means *having stalks.*

Pentas Lanceolata
Egyptian Star Cluster

This plant can be started from seeds, which are easy to buy. It comes from tropical Africa, yet grows without difficulties outdoors or in the garden room. Soft, hairy leaves and hairy stems carry the cluster of showy, inch-long flowers of five petals, hence the name: *pentas* means *five*. The color of the flowers can be white, pink, red, or lavender. It easily grows to a height of 2 or 3 feet. It is good also in a hanging basket, because some branches droop. Cuttings of partly ripened wood root better over bottom heat. It likes bright light, even sun, warmth and moisture. Keep moist. *Lanceolata* means (leaves) *tapering to a point at either end.*

Russelia Equisetiformis
Coral Plant, Fountain Plant

This plant does not have leaves. Its thin, arching branches are full of one-inch-long, bright-red, tubular flowers. The leaves are reduced to small scales. Of Mexican origin, it needs bright light and

Pentas lanceolata.

dry soil. The long, drooping branches beg to be put into a hanging basket. Cuttings taken in spring root easily in moist sand with a bottom heat of 75° F. Since Russelia does not have leaves it has to be kept dry. It is named after botanical writer Alexander Russel. *Equisetiformis* means *having form of equisetum* (horsetail plant, which has leaves reduced to scales).

Setcreasea Pallida

Every day in the morning this plant greets you with fresh, three-petaled lavender flowers. The blossom, lasting only one day, is three quarters of an inch across, growing from a boat-shaped bract at the end of runners. When the supply of blossoms in the bract is exhausted, the short branches dry up and have to be cut off. However, new, fleshy runners always grow in time with a supply of flowers.New branches grow first erect, later becoming pendant; so this plant is grown to its best advantage on a shelf or in a hanging basket. The leaves are hairy, green with purplish tint. It likes shade and to be kept moist. Cuttings root easily in sand. The name *pallida* means *pale*.

Torenia Fournieri
Wishbone Plant

Only about 12 inches tall and a fast-growing plant, named after the Swedish botanist Toren. It is grown generally as an annual. The flower has a

Setcreasea pallida.

front lip drooping down, revealing stamens and stigma. It is available in blue, white, and blue-white color of blossom. A very grateful plant. Light shade and moist soil are the requirements of this plant from Vietnam. It propagates easily from seeds and cuttings rooted in sand.

Everblooming Plants for Solid-roof Structures

Columnea Cornelian

See *Columneas,* under Everblooming Plants for Light-transmitting Roof.

Gesneria Cuneifolia

When small, this plant looks like an African violet, but is distinguished by long, shiny, narrow leaves, without stems. The leaves narrow toward the center of the plant like a wedge, and for this characteristic it bears the name *cuneifolia,* meaning *wedge-* shaped *leaves*. Only one flower is carried on each flower stalk, and flowers are produced freely. Brilliantly red, tubular, one inch-blossoms with yellow throat appear constantly. It starts blooming as a small plant.

The culture is the same as for African violets: moist soil, shade, and humidity. Propagation is from seeds and by division of older plants. Cuttings can be taken if the plant is tall enough.

It is native to islands of the Caribbean.

If the soil is acid, *gesneria* will die. Alkaline soil is a necessity. To the mixed soil for each plant should be added 2 to 3 tablespoons of calcium (for each four-inch pot). Otherwise the plant has to be watered with water-dissolved calcium (one teaspoon per quart). This treatment is less desirable.

Saintpaulia

African Violet

The first time I heard the name *African violet*

Gesneria cuneifolia.

was when a few of us children were talking about going into the meadows to pick the wild, fragrant violets. Just then two teenage girls were passing by and one of them remarked: "I would rather have African violets." Never having seen an African violet, I surmised they must be similar to the wild, fragrant ones, which were the only violets I knew as a small boy.

There is a certain similarity in blossom color of the well-known wild violet of Europe *(Viola odorata)* and the African violet *(Saintpaulia)*. And this similarity was used by Herrman Wendland, the botanist who classified and named *Saintpaulia*. He also coined a common name for it: *Usambara violet*. Since nobody knew what *Usambara* meant, it was later changed into *African violet* and is known as such worldwide.

The discovery of African violets is closely connected with the bid of Germany to become a colonial power at the end of nineteenth century. German East Africa was the last colony acquired, its territory just about the same as today's Tanzania (formerly Tanganyika). Only two years after Germany established itself in the latest colony, an

Saintpaulia 'Fire Bird.'

official of the colonial administration found in 1892 new plants never seen before. One he found near the city Tanga, by the sea, the other one on an expedition into the Usambara mountains. The long, aristocratic name of this official is used in a short form: Baron Walter von St. Paul. He sent some of the plants and seeds to his father in Germany, who shared them with his friend botanist. Within two years from introduction, *Saintpaulia* was in botanical gardens and private collections of Europe. However, it did not become popular there until after the first World War, and the United States only after World War II.

The popularity of the African violet is based on two features: its adaptability to house conditions and its constant bloom. The majority of tropical plants will not bloom in the house, requiring the warmth and humidity of an indoor garden or a greenhouse. Not even *Philodendron,* which can survive under very low light levels of a house, will bloom there. African violets come from areas of high humidity near the equator and the sea. Even the latest new species, *S. rupicola,* found in Kenya by A. B. Graf from New Jersey, was found on cliff near the sea. Hence the name *rupicola, growing on cliffs.*

All species of *Saintpaulia* have flowers in different shades of blue. Intense hybridization produced blossoms in white, pink, almost red, and two tones of colors. Besides the original species, a great selection of hybrids is available. Some catalogues list several hundred different hybrids of African violets.

Constant production of flowers is the greatest asset of *Saintpaulia.* However, it depends to a great degree on the availability of filtered light and humidity. The location of plants near a window is not sufficient enough. A north window does not have enough light in winter. South and west windows require shading from burning sun. Perhaps the best location is the east window, where *Saintpaulia* can get some morning sun. Also, the distance from a window is important. Too close to the glass in winter might be too chilly. More than three feet away from the window, the light is not of sufficient intensity. Low humidity is the most common cause of bud dropping. In an indoor garden, where humidity is high, the problem does not come up. In the house, the plants should be put on trays with pebbles and water. Also, several huddled together will maintain higher humidity for themselves. Needless to say, African violets require moist soil.

Perhaps quite critical is watering. Water splashed on leaves can cause spots. Good results are obtained with wick watering. The best is the method of some commercial growers: plants in pots stand on a layer of sand, which is daily flooded. The excess water drains away; however, dry pot and soil draw enough moisture from wet sand. This method eliminates overwatering, crown rot, and rotting of leaves. At the same time high humidity is provided.

Saintpaulia is not a perennial in the full sense. The average useful life is 2 to 3 years. Afterward some quit blooming, others slow down in production of blossoms.

Propagation is by leaf cuttings in sandy peat, for best results, under the cover, also by division of large plants.

African violets belong to the large family of *Gesneriads* and are often listed in catalogues under that heading.

Sinningia Pusilla

For description see *Gloxinia,* under Special-effect Plants for Solid-roof Structures.

23
Special-effect Plants

When a *cactus* bursts out with blossoms for Thanksgiving, the *Poinsettia* for Christmas, and *Gloxinia* for Mother's Day, we appreciate the special meaning of such plants. We like the beauty that they bring to our festivities and use the plants to convey our feelings.

People have always used flowering beauty to enhance human life. Flowers accompany all important steps in our life, joyous as well as sorrowful. Would anyone wonder if we were to include special-effect plants in the room of delight?

Special-Effect Plants for Light-Transmitting Roof Structures

Abelia Grandiflora

A shrub from the honeysuckle family, growing well in an indoor garden, also called *glossy Abelia* for its shiny leaves. The small, white flowers are pink tinted and very fragrant, blooming from June to October. *Abelia* needs good light, even sunlight, and moist soil. It is an excellent patio plant. Propagation in summer is from cuttings of green wood under cover; in fall from cuttings of mature wood. It is an insect-free plant named after Dr. Abel, a British physician in China. *Grandiflora* means *large flowered*. The country of origin is China.

Acalypha
Chenille Plant

Acalyphas are known for flowers hanging like long, chenille tassels. Coming from tropical areas, they need warmth, good light, and moist soil. Propagation is from cuttings of partly ripened wood, taken in fall or winter, in sand over bottom heat.

A. hispida (or *sanderii*) is from India. The hairy leaves are green, but the main interest are its red flowers, about 18 inches long. The variety *alba* produces white tassels. The *alba* variety wants filtered light. *Hispida* means *having bristles*.

A. wilkesiana, called *copper leaf* comes from South Pacific islands. The main attraction are leaves blotched with red, bronze, and pink. The reddish flowers are about 8 inches long.

A.'Ceylon' is a variety with curved leaves, gathered through the center, of maroon color and red, serrated edges. However, this bright coloring is maintained only in strong light or sun. When grown in the shade, the leaves revert to green and the red edges become white. It is an attractive plant either way.

Aeschynanthus

What in tropical Americas are *Columneas,* in

Acalypha 'Ceylon.'

tropical Asia are *Aeschynanthus:* vines with vividly colored, tubular, erected flowers. Some of them are called *lipstick vine,* for their peculiar growing habits of flowers, similar to the raising of lipstick from its tube. When the flower starts to grow, first appears the calyx, which is a narrow tube, growing to about one inch in height. Later, from its bottom starts to push another tube, rounded on top, bright red, overgrowing the calyx, and extending above it 2 inches or more. When fully grown, the rounded tube opens its lips.

Pollination starts another peculiarity. The pollinated ovary develops into a thin, round fruit, growing through the center of the flower to quite a length. The longest I measured was thirteen and a half inches. The ripened fruit splits lengthwise, opening four long compartments, tightly packed with seeds. Each seed is equipped with two hairs serving as wings for transportation by air movements.

Aeschynanthus when small is a nice-looking plant. But it is displayed to its best advantage in a hanging basket. Humidity, warmth, moist soil, and shade are its requirements. It propagates easily from seeds or cuttings rooted in sandy peat under cover.

A.'Black Pagoda,' a hybrid, has thick leaves marbeled maroon on the underside. The flowers are orange-yellow, born in terminal groups of 2 to 5 together.

A. lobbianus has small, bright green leaves and red flowers, emerging from a deep-maroon calyx—the real"lipstick vine." It is named for collector Thomas Lobb, who found it in Java.

A. pulcher (means *pretty*) is very similar to *A. lobbianus*.

A. 'Pullobia' is a cross between *A. pulcher* and *A. lobbianus*. It blooms several times a year with vivid red flowers. The only difference is a green calyx from which the red flower grows.

Aeschynanthus 'Pullobia.'

A. marmoratus is grown more for its dark-green leaves with yellow veins. The flowers are green splashed with chocolate. *Marmoratus* means *marbled*.

A. speciosus is a very showy and very strong grower. Bright orange flowers are up to 4 inches long. *Speciosus* means *showy*.

Aeschynanthus blooms several times a year. It takes two and half months from pollinated flower to ripened seed. By the time seeds start to spill from the pods, new flowers are forming.

Aeschynanthus belongs to the *Gesneriad* family. The name means *ashamed flower* — an allusion to the bright-red tube slowly emerging from the calyx.

Allamanda
Golden Cup

A woody vine from tropical South America, *Allamanda* can brighten up any garden room. The golden trumpets, three or more inches across, reflect from glossy, dark-green foliage of beautiful *Allamanda cathartica hendersonii* climbing on the wall. The golden cups are produced from early spring until fall. During flowering time it has to be kept moist, very moist, and fertilized often. After flowering, when vigorous growth stops, it should be kept dry. In January the supply of moisture can be again increased.

Since *Allamanda* is a vigorous grower, it does best when potted in a large pot or tub. For best flowering it needs bright light and sun. Propagation is from woody cuttings rooted in sand or vermiculite. (The name *Catharitica* reminds one of laxative qualities, when parts of plant were used for medicinal purposes).

Several other *Allamandas* are cultivated. *A. williamsii* is similar to the *cathartica* and has smaller yellow flowers. *A. violacea* is another climber with reddish-purple flowers. (The name means *violet.*) *A. neriifolia* is not a vine, but a shrub displaying golden-yellow, three-inch-long flowers, striped reddish inside. (*Neriifolia* means *leaves like oleander.*) *Allamanda* was named for Dr. Allamand, a Dutch scientist.

Amomum Cardamon
Cardamon Ginger

A member of the ginger family bearing the spicy cardamon seeds. A large plant, growing six or more feet in height, with leaves about 12 inches long. It has to be planted in a ground bed or large container. All parts are spicy when rubbed. Yellow flowers grow in clusters on stalks rising directly from the roots. Like many plants from Southeast Asia, it needs filtered light, warmth, humidity, and moist soil. During three months in winter it should be kept dry. Propagation is by seeds or division of clumps.

Anthurium

Going in a restaurant for lunch once we found on each table a vase with several *Anthuriums*. Struck by the beauty of the curious-looking flowers, my friends inquired about the name and would not believe those flowers were real, naturally grown. They suspected artificial ones. Finally, someone asked the waiter, who confirmed the plants to be real.

The brightly colored spathe of *Anthurium* is deceiving, because it is thick, leathery, shiny, and quilted, growing in an unreal, horizontal position. The white spadix, rising straight up, is a thick stalk on which are crowded tiny, indistinguishable flowers: male in the upper half, female in the lower.

The attractively colored spathe is not available in all *Anthuriums*. Generally *A. andraeanum* and *A. scherzerianum* are grown for the colorful

Anthurium andraeanum.

"blossom." Another group of *Anthuriums* is grown for its highly veined leaves.

Anthuriums are from the South American tropics and require subdued light, warmth, humidity, and moist soil. All have a tendency to "heave" or raise their central roots above the soil. It is important to keep the raised roots covered with sphagnum moss, always kept moist. Propagation is by top cuttings with several leaves and preferably with some aerial roots. The cutting can be planted directly in the pot. Propagation can also be by division of older plants. The soil should have mixed in some peat or sphagnum moss for better retaining of moisture.

Anthurium means *tail flower* — a reference to the tall spadix.

A. andraeanum comes from the rainforests of Colombia. The most showy and most grown, its flowers are suspected of being artificial. The white spadix is erect, on matured blossom slightly curved; the spathe is brightly red, coral, salmon red, or white, depending on the variety. The flowers are long lasting, even when cut. It will bloom all year if kept warm and in high humidity. The large, glossy green leaves are heart shaped. This is the most desirable of all *Anthuriums*.

A. scherzerianum is easily distinguished from *A. andraeanum*. The leaves are long and narrow, the white spadix is curled in the pigtail fashion. For this peculiarity the common name is *pigtail plant*. The spathe is colored in shades of red and pink. Although it blooms intermittently throughout the year, its blooming seasons are spring and summer. A variety, *A. scherzerianum rothschildianum,* has red or reddish spathe speckled with white.

Anthurium will not bloom if all the soil in the pot (even the bottom) is not moist.

Anthuriums that are grown for beautiful leaves have insignificant flowers: the spathe is smaller and mostly green, with shades of yellow and red.

A. crystallinum has emerald-green, heart-shaped leaves veined in silver. The band along the veins is made of tiny silver crystals, glittering in strong light, especially when observed in sunshine. Leaves are 8 inches or longer. It is almost identical to *A. magnificum,* also from Colombia.

A. clarinervium is very similar to the two preceding ones. A smaller plant with quite thick leaves, and comes from Mexico.

Another *anthurium* from Colombia is *A. warrocqueanum,* called *Queen Anthurium.* The velvety green leaves with silver veins can grow to a length of 36 inches. It is a climber, needing support.

Avoid spraying all anthuriums with Malathion.

Ardisia Crispa
Coral Berry

This is a compact, bushy plant with dark-green leaves and bright-red berries. The blossoms are either white or reddish, growing in clusters, and developing in winter into red berries, lasting until late spring. The leaves have scalloped edges, which are thickened. It is somethimes called *A. crenulata,* and needs some shade and moderately moist soil. Propagation is from seeds, extracted from berries and washed, sown in winter time; also from half-ripened wood with the help of bottom heat. Comes from China-Japan. *Ardisia* in Greek means *point; crispa: crisp, curled; crenulata: scalloped.*

Aristolochia Elegans
Calico Flower

Some members of the *Aristolochia* family grow in Eastern sections the United States and are known as Dutchman's pipe and Virginia snakeroot. *Aristolochia elegans,* native to Brazil, is grown for large, unusually shaped flowers. The blossom tube is yellow-green on the outside; the flared-out section is purplish with white markings. A climber, it can be grown easily in pots. It blooms all summer and rests in winter. After blooming, when leaves are drying, it should be cut back, leaving a stump 6 to 10 inches long, and watered sparingly. In spring, with active growth starting it should be watered more and kept moderately moist. It needs good light. Older plants bloom more profusely. It is an insect-free plant.

Azaleas

Azaleas are the most beautiful plants from the north temperate zone. The ones native to the United States and Europe are deciduous; those from the Orient are evergreen and were developed into

Ardisia crispa.

hybrids suitable for pot culture and widely sold as gift plants.

The hybrids of florist *Azaleas* are of three groups. *Kurume* is named for a city in southern Japan where it originated and has blossoms about an inch and a half across and in great profusion. *Indica azaleas* were crossed in Belgium using Kurume hybrids and Chinese species. This group has the largest flowers, three inches across, but fewer blooms. In the USA were developed *Rutherfordiana*' hybrids, using *Kurume* and *Indica Azaleas,* to produce superior quality plants with blossoms two and a half inches, which have the wealth of flowers of *Kurume* and large-size blossoms of *Indicas*. Colors of these hybrids are white, pink, salmons, and red, some in two-color combinations, a few with purple splashes.

Azaleas can be successfully rebloomed every year. Summer can be spent outside in light shade. The one problem is watering. *Azaleas* should be watered daily, but outside are easily forgotten; often they dry up completely. Mine survive the heat in the garden room near the discharge of the evaporative cooler, where movement of cool air keeps them healthy. The winter bloom is forced by cool temperatures of 50° - 60° F. It is always possible to find a corner in the garden room near glass, where such a temperature is available.

The beauty of *Azaleas* is not only in the individual blossom, but also in the profusion of flowers, which often hide the foliage. To produce such an amount of blossoms, the *Azalea* needs large quantities of water. When in flower, watering twice a day is not too much. If they do not get enough water, the dropping of leaves tells. In the same manner *Azaleas* rebel against insufficient light. Bright light, with some mild early morning or late afternoon sun is necessary.

If you buy or receive an *Azalea* it is easy to notice how light the pot is. The pot is filled not with the soil, but with peat moss, for two reasons: peat holds moisture and is the source of an acid medium, which is essential for the *Azalea*. To keep acidity, it is necessary to apply aluminum sulfate, or iron sulfate, fertilize with Acid Grow, or simply dust some garden sulphur on top the peat moss in the pot. When repotting, the *Azalea* should be put into pure peat moss, which is acid, or a mixture of sand (one part) and peat (three parts).

Azaleas also need more iron than other plants. Iron deficiency, called chlorosis, is apparent in yellowing of the leaves, which drop off. Chlorosis can be corrected by iron chelate dissolved in water and used at the time of watering.

Propagation is by cuttings of half-ripened wood rooted in a sandy peat moss with bottom heat. Cuttings should be taken between June and November.

Begonia Dichroa

This Cane-type *Begonia* has large, glossy green leaves and clusters of two-tone, bright-orange flowers. It needs warmth, high humidity, and plenty of moisture. It is easily propagated from cuttings rooted in water or good rooting medium. It blooms as a small plant. For best results keep moist. *Dichroa* means *of two colors* (flowers).

Bougainvillea

The discovery of *Bougainvilleas* is connected

Begonia dichroa.

with the first voyage around the world by a woman. In 1768 it was not possible for a woman to undertake such travel on primitive and dangerous ships. They simply were not permitted to embark on a ship going around the world, which took more than a year.

When a young french girl, Jeanne Baret, decided that she wanted to be the first woman to travel around the world, she had to do it in the disguise of a man. The botanist in the expedition of Captain Bougainville was sympathetic and hired her as his helper. Her true identity was revealed only when she was almost kidnapped on the island of Tahiti by a native chief, who in his natural instinct was not fooled by the disguise of the young Jeanne.*

The *Bougainvilleas* were found on the same expedition near Rio de Janeiro and named in honor of the captain. These prolific vines of the tropics will also grow in an indoor garden. If planted in a ground bed, it will cover a wall very soon; when put into a pot, it will not rebel and will be content, growing and blooming well. The small, yellow flowers always grow in groups of three, each one being attached to one colorful bract (modified leaf). The splendor of *Bougainvillea* is in the colorful bracts. However, the purpose of this glory is very prosaic: if the flowers are pollinated, each bract serves as a paper-tin parachute to carry the seeds over distances.

Bright light and sun are necessary for flowering. In the garden room *Bougainvillea* will bloom intermittently throughout the year, depending on the available sun. The soil should be kept dry.

Perhaps the nicest color is provided by *B. Buttiana* 'Barbara Karst' with bright purplish-red bracts. *B 'California Gold'* has dark-yellow bracts. *Bougainvilleas* with white variegated foliage do not provide such an effect, since the attention is attracted to the foliage more than to the colorful bracts. One such plant is *B. Harrisii* having purple bracts, seldom in bloom. The variegated foliage is a reward for proper care.

Cuttings of half-ripened wood will root under cover with help of bottom heat.

*Based on a story in the book by A.W. Anderson, *How We Got Our Flowers*. Copyright © 1966 by Dover Publications, Inc. Used with permission.

Bouvardia

Many wedding bouquets contain fragrant, white flowers carrying four petals on slender, two-inch long white tubes. The white flowers, having orange blossom scent, are *Bouvardia longiflora*. It blooms normally in early summer and later in winter. For winter blooming it should be exposed to sun. Bud forming is best at a night temperature of 55-60° F. For that reason it should be kept in a cooler corner. *Bouvardia longiflora* is propagated from tip cuttings taken in winter. *Longiflora* means *long flower*.

B. ternifolia is red blooming; the tube is much shorter than *B. longiflora*. In flower most of the year, with heavy blooming in summer and fall. Propagation is from root cuttings in June. One-inch-long sections of root are put in the pot and barely covered with soil. The regular soil mixture then has to be kept moist. Temperature should be 60° F. or more. Besides the red-flowering *Bouvardia* is also available white and pink varieties. *Ternifolia* means *leaves in threes*.

Bouvardias are shrubs 2 to 3 feet tall and insect free. Coming from the Mexico-Texas area, they need moderately dry soil. For summer bloom it is best to plunge pots in the soil outdoors in a sunny place. Named for French royal gardener Bouvard.

Canna

The beautiful, large flowered *Canna* with huge leaves is a nice addition to any indoor garden. Native to tropical America, *Canna* prospers better indoors than in cold climates outdoors, where cool nights and short summers do not allow for proper development.

The best place for *Cannas* is next to glass. However, they must be protected from direct sun by curtains, otherwise the sun will burn the delicate blossoms. It is peculiar, since outside *Cannas* thrive in sun — but in the open. The last condition is not supplied in a garden room, especially when the blower is inoperative, like on sunny but cold days in spring or fall.

Cannas grow from large, tuberous rhizomes, which can be planted directly into the ground bed. From then on you do not have to worry about propagation. Before one strong stalk is done flowering, a new one is already rising from the tuber.

After the flowering of any stalk, which takes several weeks, when no new buds appear or can be felt in the sheet, the stalk should be cut off near the ground. Otherwise the leaves will become breeding grounds for spider mites. These pests are fond of *Cannas,* although they cannot damage the large, thick leaves. The best precaution is to spray *Cannas* often.

Cannas have been hybridized so intensively and so long that the original plant is unknown today. For that reason *Cannas* cannot be propagated from seeds. Plants grown from such seeds will have large leaves, but the flowers will be small and of muddy, unclear colors.

Since *Cannas* are very active plants, producing large leaves and flowers, they need frequent fertilizing and good watering. When such care is provided, *Cannas* can be active all year. However, being planted near the outside wall, the severe winter cold will prevent some of them from growing lavishly, but with warmer spring temperatures will burst into life again. Their partial dormancy is short, generally from December to March.

Carissa Grandiflora
Natal plum

The common name of *Carissa* indicates the land of origin: Natal in South Africa. The word *plum* points to the edible red fruit, egg-shaped, 1 to 2 inches long. The white flowers are fragrant and in strong light and sun will bloom all year. Red Fruit,

Citrus mitis.

white blossoms, and glossy green leaves make a colorful combination. In Florida, *Carissa* is sheared into impenetrable hedges, due to the forked spines. Propagation is from seeds or cuttings of ripened wood rooted in the early fall. Soil has to be kept moderately moist. The name *Carissa* is of unknown origin.

Citrus

Northerners are fascinated with the orange. This fascination was the reason for starting indoor gardens and has not diminished yet. Miniature oranges and lemons are kept in pots and tubs in houses of severe climate, as well as large trees in greenhouses and conservatories.

Several varieties of *Citrus* trees are available for indoor culture, ornamental and edible. All have handsome, glossy green foliage, white fragrant flowers, and fruit, which especially in the orange provides a nice color complement to the green leaves. The popularity of *Citrus* is supported by their adaptability: they are not particular about temperature—they are satisfied with 50° F and higher; they do not require high humidity or copious moisture; they want bright light and if possible sun. However, they have one requirement: iron. Iron deficiency is shown by a large number of yellowing leaves, which drop off. That situation can be easily corrected by applications of chelated iron, like Sequestrene.

To obtain an abundance of fruit, the blossoms of orange and lemon trees grown inside must be pollinated with a brush.

The most suitable varieties of *Citrus* are:

C. mitis, 'Calamondin orange' from the Philippines. If grown in a ground bed it will make a nice tree up to nine feet tall, with blooms and fruit all year, especially if sun is available. The fruit are small oranges, one inch round, sour but good for jam or when eaten with sugar. *Mitis* means *mild.*

C. taitensis, 'Tahiti orange.' Does not come from Tahiti, but from South China. It is ornamental and good for pot culture, since it grows only 2 to 3 feet tall. White flowers, pinkish on the outside, appear in January and are followed by inch-and-a-half fruit, which will stay on the tree very long. The fruit is very tart.

C. 'Meyeri' is a hybrid of lemon and sweet orange, with lavender-tinted white flowers. It produces a good quality of lemons all year.

C. limon 'Ponderosa,' "American wonder lemon," is a hybrid originated in Maryland bearing huge size lemons, only a few at a time, averaging two pounds.

C. aurantifolia, 'Key lime,' bears small, round limes that turn yellow at maturity. It fruits year round. *Aurantifolia* means *golden leaved.*

C. aurantifolia, 'Persian lime,' has large limes of very good quality, which stay green. It bears fruit all year.

Citrus trees like light soil, high in sand. Overwatering is dangerous only with limes, which rot easily. Propagation is by cuttings of ripened wood rooted in sandy soil or sandy peat, deeply inserted into propagating medium.

Chrysanthemum

The oldest flower in continuous cultivation, the Chrysanthemum is the national flower of China and Japan, where it was grown for more than 3,000 years. It is the flower of fall — however, not exclusively, since it was found that it can be brought into bloom at any time of the year. The requirement is complete darkness for twelve or more hours daily for a duration of three weeks. (Florists achieve this by covering mums with dark cloth over wires stretched above plants.)

Cuttings for many named varieties can be purchased or taken from existing plants. Rooting is easy in moist sand. For November bloom, cuttings should be rooted in June. Cuttings rooted in fall will bloom five months later. Rooted cuttings, when several are transplanted into a pot, should be pinched for bushier growth. No pinching should be done 100 days before the wanted bloom. Buds form in great profusion and the undesirable ones should be pinched out (disbudded) and only one or two left on each branch for large flowers.

Treat mums as annuals. If left for another year, they will bloom well; however, by that time you will have straggly plants shooting runners on nearby plants in search for support. It is best to leave mums in pots after flowering and in June to take cuttings for the next season. *Chrysanthemums* need all possible light for development of full flowers. If light is insufficient they form irregular blossoms. And, of course, mums are

Clerodendrum thomsonae.

very thirsty. Frequent watering is necessary. The name *Chrysanthemum* means *golden flower*.

Clerodendrum Thomsonae
Bleeding Heart Vine

This plant can be grown as a vine or a shrub. Clerodendrum blooms on new wood, so if pruned sufficiently it will bloom twice a year with striking flowers. Blossoms are not only exquisite but their development is also interesting. First appears a pure white calyx that looks like a Chinese lantern. Later the calyx is graced with a bright-red corolla through which start to grow long stamens. It blooms in winter and in summer with long-lasting flowers. It has to be grown in good light and needs moist soil, especially during flowering. Its land of origin is tropical West Africa. Propagation is from cuttings of semi-ripened wood rooted in sand.

Cobea Scandens

Cup-and-saucer Vine; Cathedral Bells

A fast growing climber. During the summer it will grow easily to a length of 25 feet. The white or violet flower is a calyx — a tube— about 2 inches long; at the base are flared out green sepals, giving an appearance of a cup sitting on a saucer. After flowering it should be cut down, since all leaves dry up anyway. It is generally grown as an annual. Propagation is from seeds, which should be soaked for 24 hours before planting or notched for easier sprouting. It is insect-free plant requiring bright light. Although *Cobea* is native to Mexico, the soil should be kept moist. It is named after botanist Father Cobo.

Coffea Arabica
Arabian Coffee Tree

The Coffee tree! Curiosity and expectation are in these words. How does the tree and *Coffee* bean look?

In a pot located in the house, the *Coffee* tree grows slowly and makes a handsome foliage plant. Its green, shiny leaves can brighten any area, but in an indoor garden, placed in a ground bed or large tub, it will shoot up into a real tree. High humidity and freedom of roots will help it to reach a height of nine feet in four years. In the third year some white blossoms will appear. If promptly pollinated with a brush, they will develop into green berries, changing to red with maturity and dark red when ripened.

The red berries are called *cherries* in trade. Each contains two green beans, the source of coffee. However, it is not so easy to release the beans from the *cherries*. The best way is to pick from the tree the dark red berries, and lay them anywhere on flat surface for two days. This is called *fermentation,* during which the cherries will get soft; slight squeezing will yield two green beans. For trade, the beans have to be dried to a hard gloss, to make handling of *Coffee* beans easy. However, such drying kills all viability of seed.

When observing young *Coffee* seedlings sprouting under a *Coffee* tree in a conservatory, a person is led to believe that germination of *Coffee* seeds is easy. This is true only under certain conditions. The best conditions are: planting seeds right after releasing from berries and maintaining a temperature in the seed bed at 82° F. Under such conditions the first seedlings will emerge after four weeks. It was the shortest time I was able to get seedlings, with germination approaching 100 percent. At a temperature of 68 - 70° F, with fresh seeds, the germination period will be 6 to 8 weeks. The older and dryer the seeds, the longer it will take for seedlings to emerge and the lower the percentage of germination.

Shade, humidity, and moist soil are necessary for growth and bloom. Yellowing of leaves is quite common. It indicates that the *Coffee* tree needs chelated iron. Sometimes even this treatment fails for a simple reason: *Coffee* needs more potash than other plants. Fertilizing with potash or complete fertilizer high in potash will correct the deficiency.

The *Coffee* tree does not come from Arabia as the name would indicate. Its native land is Ethiopia, where wild *Coffee* trees in forests can still be found.

Columnea

For introduction to *Columneas* see section "Everblooming plants." Besides everblooming, many *Columneas* bloom at different times of the

Coffea arabica Fruits.

Columnea 'Ontario.'

Cuphea platycentra.

year. Some have even the added attraction of colorful leaves.

C. gloriosa (means *glorious)* lives up to its name. The leaves are covered with reddish hair and the beauty is enhanced by large, 3 inch-tall flowers, standing erect on trailing vines. It blooms profusely in winter and spring and outside of this period it always has some flowers. It requires humidity, moist soil, and warmth.

Similar is *C. hirta,* having almost red leaves and flowering even more profusely. *Hirta* means *hairy.*

C. microphyla has very small leaves, hence the name, meaning *small leaved.* The half-inch, bronzy leaves covered with hairs are almost lost next to large, three inch tall, red blossoms. It is spring blooming.

C.'Stavanger' is a Norwegian hybrid of *C. microphyla.* It retains the small, half-inch leaves, which are green, but the flowers are even larger than *microphyla's.*

C. 'Ontario' has large glossy leaves and yellow-orange flowers. Blooms almost continually. Keep it moderately moist.

Cuphea Platycentra
Cigar Flower

This is a small plant laden with one-inch long tubular flowers, in bright red color, having the edge black and white. The particular coloring of the edge of the blossom led to the name *cigar flower.* It is a very grateful plant, growing and blooming well in good light. Easy to start from seeds, or cuttings rooted in moist sand. Its land of origin is Mexico, which indicates the need of warmth and sun. Soil should be kept moderately moist. It is an insect-free plant, grown generally as an annual. *Platycentra* means *broad centered.*

Episcia

Episcias are distant relatives of African violets. In nature they are separated by great distances.The home of *Episcias* is the tropics of Central and South America, whereas African violets (*Saintpaulias*) live in tropical East Africa. Both belong to the *Gesneriad* family and have many common traits. The name means *of shade,* describing *Episcias* love for shade. Although *Episcias* want shade, they still need more light and humidity than African violets.

From nature *Episcias* were gifted with great diversity of leaf and blossom color. The coppery color of the leaves is dominant in some species; others have leaves deep green, plain, or silver veined. Flowers have greater diversity: red, orange-red, lavender, yellow, or pure white. Hybridization did not bring any new colors of blossoms, but extended the variety of leaf coloring. With bright and colorful leaves *Episcias* try to stay in competition with African violets, although they are losing on two counts: a limited blooming period of 3 to 8 months (depending on variety), and the need for higher humidity (minimum 40 percent). That makes them less-ideal house plants.

The first *Episcia* introduced into cultivation was *E. cupreata* (which means *coppery*), named so for its copper color of leaves. It is still the most grown of *Episcias,* either as species or in many hybrids, like *E. 'Chocolate soldier.'* The leaves of hybrids have silver veins or silver areas. Flowers are mostly orange-red. A sport of *E. cupreata*, not even resembling one, is *'Tropical topaz'* from the Panama Canal zone. Vivid yellow flowers and bright green leaves appear not to have anything in common with the copper-leaved species and hybrids. The 'Tropical Topaz' does not flower very profusely. The longest flowering period belongs to the hybrids of *E. cupreata 'variegata'* and *Viridifoia,'* which bloom almost all year.

E. lilacina and its hybrids have lilac-colored flowers and dark bronze leaves.

E. reptans (means *creeping)* and its hybrids have highly veined and blotched leaves; flowers are red.

Plain green, small leaves has *E. dianthiflora,* named so for its pure white blossoms with fringed edges, resembling the flower of *Dianthus* (carnation). Blooming time is late spring and summer. This *Episcia* is an exception, wanting to have soil moderately dry. The small leaves are thick, indicating the water storing capability.

Episcias are very sensitive to low temperatures. At 55° F most of them start to "freeze," lose leaves, and go dormant. An exception again is *E. dianthiflora,* capable of withstanding 45° F. Recovery can be achieved by putting *Episcias* into warm temperatures again. Visiting a commercial greenhouse once, I noticed a number of *Episcias*

Episcia cupreata 'Chocolate Soldier'

growing under the bench and spreading in sandy soil. Those *E. 'Chocolate Soldiers'* growing in this manner on the north side of the greenhouse puzzled me, because the outdoor temperature that day was—8° F. I did not understand, how they could survive on that spot. So I returned to investigate and found two large heating pipes almost sinking into the sand and forming a barrier of heat between the cold north wall and a colony of happily sprawling *Episcias*.

Propagation is very easy from cuttings in soil or sand. In fact, it often happens that a runner of *Episcia* touches soil in another pot and sinks roots there. It is then easy to cut off such a rooted section from the mother plant, lift it with roots from the soil, and put it in a pot of its own.

Euphorbia Fulgens
Scarlet Plume

This is a winter-flowering relative of *Poinsettia,* from which it differs in two ways: the leaves are willow like, narrow, and dark green. Secondly, the small flowers do not force the leaves to change color during flowering. However, the small flowers have another way to attract attention. Being only a half inch in diameter, they grow close together on gracefully arching branches. The orange-red color of the blossom reflects brightly from the dark leaves.

Although not as showy as *Poinsettia,* scarlet plume is very attractive. The culture and propagation is the same as for *Poinsettia,* even if it is not so touchy. It will grow well in shade with moderately dry soil. *Fulgens* means *shining.*

Euphorbia Pulcherrima
Poinsettia

When Joel R. Poinsett returned in 1829 from his service as U.S. ambassador to Mexico, he brought back an unusual plant. Mexicans called it "Flor de

Euphorbia fulgens.

Noche Buena'' — flower of Holy Night. Poinsett could not foresee that the same plant—*Euphorbia pulcherrima* — would be named after him and that at Christmas time it would adorn millions of homes in the United States.

Poinsettia is a nice foliage plant during the year. But when the days get short and the night extends its darkness for 12 hours or more, *Euphorbia pulcherrima* sets the buds. This happens in October. After several weeks the new green leaves growing just below the tiny buds, start to change color. Depending on the variety, the topmost cluster of leaves will be red, pink, white, or white blotched with pink.

The newly developed *Poinsettias* are more suitable for dark and dry rooms of an average house and are longer lasting. After the bloom fades away *Poinsettia* can be kept as a foliage plant. It will grow well and tall, with the lower leaves dropping off, which is natural. July or August is the time to take cuttings. Any section can be used for cutting — except the hard woody one — even sections without leaves. The cuttings should have at least two nodes and should be put into a plastic bag at once to prevent wilting.

After the milky juice, oozing from the cut, sets — which takes several hours — cuttings can be put into the rooting medium. It is possible to put them directly into the soil. However, stem rot will take its toll unless the potting soil is very sandy. The best is to root cuttings in sand. To avoid stem rot, some commercial growers use a one-inch cube of Styrofoam for each cutting; cubes are set on moist sand. When roots grow through the Styrofoam, the cutting with the cube is transplanted directly into the pot.

During rooting time the flat with cuttings should be set on some elevated surface, table or shelf, to be maintained at room temperature. If set on floor, where it is cooler, the rooting process will take two months or more.

For setting the buds the *Poinsettia* has two requirements: cooler night temperature and darkness. The temperature must be below 65°F at night. The darkness must be uninterrupted for at least 12 hours. If the darkness is broken by light, even flashlight, the flowering will be delayed.

The formation of full crowns of modified leaves around the small flowers depends on the brightness of the daylight. Any long period of cloudy and dull days endangers the fullness of crowns. Commercial growers, who must produce nice, saleable plants, turn light above *Poinsettias* on cloudy days. In an indoor garden of lean-to construction, *Poinsettias* must be located so as to have light from more than one side. Otherwise the modified leaves will not develop properly on the side facing the solid wall. In this respect white *Poinsettias* are much better plants, easily forming full crowns.

Poinsettias should be kept moderately dry.

Euphorbia is named after Euphorbus, the physician to a king of Numidia in North Africa, who lived in the time just before the coming of Jesus Christ.

Pulcherrima means *very pretty*.

Fuchsia

The "Ladies' Eardrops" have beautiful blossoms. No wonder they commanded high prices in the eigthteenth century. *Fuchsia coccineas* was brought from South America by a sailor to his mother in England, who kept it in a window. Soon it was recognized as a new species by the owner of a leading British nursery and bought by him for a sum equivalent to a year and half wages of a skilled worker. The rooted cuttings of the same plant were sold, each for one weeks wages.*

In the nineteenth century, *Fuchsias* were very popular. Over fifteen hundred varieties were in cultivation. Despite intense hybridizing, perhaps the nicest of all is *Fuchsia magellanica* from Peru. The bright red sepals and deep blue petals form a beautiful combination of hanging blossoms. Most *Fuchsias* bloom in spring and summer, others in winter, and some are everblooming. The tall-growing *F. 'Rufus'* with bright-red blossoms, and *F. 'Swanley Yellow*,' the hanging basket type with orange red flowers, stay in bloom all year.

Fuchsias like a cool, moist, and shady location. Summers should be spent outside, since an indoor garden would be too hot for them. The exception is *F.'Gartenmeister Bohnstedt,'* a German hybrid, which is a proven house plant. It will take the heat of a garden room without slowdown in blooming. It is called "Honeysuckle fuchsia." Salmon- colored tubular flowers grow in clusters and are complemented with red-veined, dark green leaves.

From November to January *Fuchsias* are semidormant. More active growth starts with longer days in February. Soil should be kept moderately dry. Softwood cuttings root easily in moist sand. Berries of *Fuchsia* are edible and suitable for making jelly, which is utilized in the warmer climate in California. Named in honor of German botanist Fuchs.

*Based on a story in the book by A.W. Anderson, *How We Got Our Flowers*. Copyright © 1966 by Dover Publications, Inc. Used with permission.

Hibiscus Rosa-Sinensis
Chinese Hibiscus

Hibiscus, the familiar plant of the tropics, is a gift of East Indies and China. It is known for its huge, very attractive flowers lasting only one day. The single form is especially showy with the simplicity of large petals and the staminal column rising from its center. The double flowers are smaller, about four inches, full of ruffles and without staminal column. The predominating colors are red, pink, and yellow, some are streaked with rose.

The best blooming is the cultivar Scarlet, which has single flowers. One variety, *H. cooperi,* is grown for its colorful foliage. The dark green leaves are variegated with white, pink, and red, but the scarlet blossoms are small.

Hibiscus needs bright light, sun if possible, and moderately moist soil. Propagation is from cuttings of ripened wood deeply inserted into propagating medium.

Hibiscus is an old latin name for *Hollyhock,* which belongs to the same family as Chinese *Hibiscus*.

Ixora

Ixoras grow in tropical Asia, where they are very much loved. In fact they are so popular that the name of one god of southern India was transferred to these plants. Small, four-petal flowers

Hibiscus rosa-sinensis 'Red Gold.'

Ixora macrothyrsa 'Super King.'

are grouped together, forming heads similar to those of the *Geranium*. Hence, *Ixora* is often called "Jungle geranium."

Its colors are gay: white, pink, salmon, red, orange, yellow. Colorful heads in some hybrids are enormous: six or seven inches across. The cultural requirements are simulation of the tropics: warm and humid atmosphere, bright light, and moist soil. *Ixora* often suffers from iron deficiency and should receive applications of fertilizer with iron content or iron chelate to maintain healthy, green foliage. Good *ixoras* for cultivation are:

I. coccinea, which has large clusters of deep-red flowers and shiny leaves. *Coccinea* means *red*.

I. 'colei' is a hybrid well known in the past century and now newly introduced. It has large, seven-inch balls of white flowers. Best growth is in partial shade.

I. 'Frances Perry' has medium-size heads of rich, yellow color. This is a new hybrid.

I. macrothyrsa comes from Sumatra. It is called "King *Ixora*" for its large leaves and huge clusters of rosy-red flowers. *Macrothyrsa* means *large-clustered flower*.

I. macrothyrsa 'Super King' has large, leathery leaves on stout canes that are topped with huge, six-inch balls of orange-red flowers. Although *Ixoras* are slow growing, the *Super King* starts flowering while still small.

For flower production, the soil ball must be continually moist. When watering, the water must leak from under the pot and the excess must be poured away.

Cuttings of young wood have to be rooted under cover and with the help of bottom heat (about 80°F.).

Jacobinia carnea.

The name *Ixora* is a corrupted form of name *Iswara,* which is the god Siva, the supreme god in the Hindu pantheon.

Jacobinia Carnea
Brazilian plume

The *Jacobinia carnea* is sometimes called *Justicia magnifica* — a name that would better describe the greatness of this plant. The large flower head is formed by two-inch blossoms, cascading one upon another into globular form. The color of these magnificent globes is the color of flesh; hence the name *carnea,* which means *flesh* colored. The satiny leaves are about 6 inches on a shrub several feet tall. It blooms in summer. Soil should be kept moderately moist. Propagation is from cuttings rooted in moist sand. It is named after the town of Jacobinia in Brazil, the land of origin.

Kalanchoe Blossfeldiana
Christmas Kalanchoe

Small mound plants, covered with bright red flowers are seen often around Christmas time. Actually this used to be the ''Christmas plant'' until *Poinsettia* started to reign in every household. *Kalanchoe* has something in commom with *Poinsettia,*: both are short-day plants. Blooming normally in January and February, it can be brought into bloom by short-day treatment under dark covering. If a blooming *Kalanchoe* is wanted for Christmas, it should be put under a cover for at least 12 hour nights from the beginning of September until the buds are set — which takes about four weeks.

Kalanchoe blossfeldiana needs bright light, even sun. It should be kept dry; watering once a week is sufficient. Propagation is very easy from seeds, formed in large quantities, since the flowers are self-pollinating. Cuttings also root very easily in sand. This plant can be carried from year to year.

Several hybrids are available. These can be recognized by large, thick leaves and clusters of blossoms on tall stems. Depending on the cultivar the flowers are red, orange, or yellow.

Avoid spraying with Malathion.

Kalanchoe Pinnata
Air Plant; Miracle leaf

This plant is cultivated not for the beauty of its leaves or blossoms, but for the curious way of self-propagation. On the matured leaves will grow plantlets. This will happen also on a leaf pinned on a curtain, or better yet pinned down on continually moist sand. From the scallops of plain green leaf small plants will start to grow which can be readily put in a pot.

Bright light or sunshine and dry soil are the requirements of this curiosity. Avoid spraying with Malathion.

Kalanchoe Tomentosa
Panda Plant

This plant is like a child; cute when little. Plump

Kalanchoe tomentosa.

Kohleria 'Rongo.'

leaves, covered with short, white hair are soft to touch and chocolate markings on the edge of the leaves make it adorable. When panda plant grows older it becomes elongated, plump leaves are flattened and the brown coloring is not so pronounced. Fortunately, it propagates easily so it is possible to always enjoy little plants. Healthy leaves are simply laid on moist sand and soon cute little plantlets appear where the leaf was cut off. Sun, bright light and spare watering are required. *Tomentosa* means *hairy*. Avoid spraying with Malathion.

Kohleria Rongo

Kohlerias grow from scaly rhizomes, requiring rest in winter. The hybrid *Rongo* has exceptional vitality, carrying on without the rest. It blooms even as a small plant with pretty, one-inch-long flowers in pink color, with a dark design on the flared-out tube. It is prolific not only in blossoms, but also, the pot is soon filled with rhizomes, from which rise new plants. Rhizomes can be used for propagation also. Even the tip cutting, full of blossoms will root, without losing flowers. The dark-green leaves have brown-black areas along the veins. *Kohlerias* were named in honor of J. M. Kohler, a teacher from Switzerland.

Medinilla Magnifica

This large shrub from the Philippines has one-foot-long, glossy green leaves with ivory veins. Its flowers, in clusters twelve inches long, are of carmine color and bracts are pink. It needs warmth, high humidity, filtered light, and plenty of moisture. It is named for the governor of Marianas Islands, Jose de Medinilla. If shaded too much, it will not bloom. It propagates by cuttings of half-ripened wood with bottom heat. It takes over four weeks to root. *Magnifica* means *magnificent*.

Mimosa Pudica
Sensitive Plant; Touch-me-not

When U.S. Armed Forces reentered the Philippines at the end of World War II, on many occasions it was easy for them to follow the retreating Japanese. The featherlike leaves of the Sensitive plant remained folded long enough to betray the path of the retreating enemy.

Mimosa pudica displays the unusual ability to fold its tiny leaflets when touched; if shocked, the leaves carrying stalks bend down. After 20 to 30 minutes they return into normal position. A curious plant, it fascinates children and adults alike. It grows very easily from seeds. The small purple flowers are self-pollinating. Generally grown as an annual, it is a perennial in its native Brazil; it is now spread throughout the tropics, where it has become a weed. It needs strong light and moist soil. *Mimosa* means *Mimic*. *Pudica* means *bashful*.

Murraya Exotica
Orange Jessamine

Orange-red berries next to white fragrant flowers are not found on many plants. *Murraya exotica* is one of few to carry both, since it blooms several times a year. It is a very nice tropical plant with small, glossy leaflets and blossoms of jasmine fragrance. It grows to a height of several feet and needs warmth, good light, and moist soil — as would be expected of a plant from India. Cuttings of ripened wood root in sandy peat under cover with the help of bottom heat. If seed is used for propagation it has to be sown immediately after picking the berries from the plant. It is named for English editor J. A. Murray. This plant is sometimes listed as *Murraea exotica*.

Passiflora
Passion Flower

One of the most interesting ways of naming a plant is as follows: The early missionaries arriving in South America used the ever-present Passion flower as a teaching aid. The complicated blossom structure of *Passiflora* offered many opportunities for explaining and memorizing the Passion and Crucifixion of Jesus Christ. The greenish petals represented the ten apostles, the white, blue and purple rays of the corona was the crown of thorns; the five antherns were reminders of the wounds; the three stigmas were similar to the nails; the coiled tendrils were the whips of flagellation; and the five-lobed leaves were the hands of the soldiers.

Strobilanthes dyerianus

Aglaonema commutatum 'White Rajah'

Hibiscus rosa-sinensis 'Red Gold'

Schlumbergera bridgesii

Passiflora alato-caerulea.

The blossoms of the Passion flower are unique. Although lasting only one day, the rapidly growing vine supplies them spring and summer. Strings and wires facilitate climbing. *Passiflora* can easily grow thirty feet in eight months. In September it should be cut down, since most of the leaves dry up anyway. After a rest of a few months it will start to climb again.

Some Passion flowers have edible fruit for which they are cultivated in the tropics. One of our fruit drinks contains the juice of *Passiflora* fruit. Being a tropical plant, the Passion flower requires warmth, humidity, bright light, and an abundance of moisture when not resting.

A number of Passion flowers are available. The original one, *P. caerulea,* has blue flowers and five-lobed leaves (*caerulea* means *blue*). Its hybrid, *P. alato-caerulea,* called *pfordtii,* is very showy, with fragrant flowers. *P. coccinea* and *P. racemosa* are red blooming. *P. edulis* and *P. quadrangularis* have edible fruit, up to ten inches long. One Passion flower has ornamental leaves: *P. trifasciata* with yellow flowers makes a colorful display with three-lobed leaves marked pink and silver along purple veins.

Plumbago Capensis
Leadwort

Among the tropical plants, there are few with blue flowers. Although *Plumbago* is a straggly plant, it is welcome in the garden room for its blue, foxlike blossoms. It does best in a hanging basket, not only because it gets the bright light, which it needs, but also because it has freedom for the outstretched branches. The azure-blue flowers appear several times a year, after a rest of a few weeks. When the straggly branches are cut back, flowering is more vigorous. *Plumbago* should be kept moist. Cuttings of young shoots root in a mixture of sand and peat moss under cover of glass or plastic. Best rooting is in February or August. There is also a white variety, called *Alba,* of this plant from South Africa's Cape of Good Hope.

Plumbago was used as a remedy for lead poisoning, hence its name, which means *lead.*

Punica Granatum
Pomegranate

"Your cheeks are like halves of pomegranate," says the bridegroom to his bride in the Song of Songs. The pomegranate is mentioned several times in this beautiful poem. Besides using the pomegranate as an example of beauty, its utility as tasteful fruit is recalled in other books of the Old Testament.

It was a well-known fruit cultivated by all the nations in the Orient. Romans learned to know it from Carthaginians in North Africa. The slang name Romans used for a Carthaginian was *punicus,* and thus was named the new discovery: *malum punicum — punic apple.* Another name was also used: *malum granatum* — seed apple — for its many seeds. This last name was then translated into french: *pomme granate.*

Used now more as an ornamental than utility tree, pomegranate is grown for its trumpet-shaped, scarlet flowers and bright red fruit, sharply contrasting against the green foliage. *Punica granatum* grows to a maximum height of 20 feet in the wild. It is often grown in conservatories. More suitable for an indoor garden is *P. granatum nana* (dwarf pomegranate), a slow growing shrub, reaching ultimately six feet. It blooms intermittently all year and bears normal-sized fruit.

Pomegranate needs strong light, even sun, and moist soil. Propagation is by cuttings of both hard and soft wood with bottom heat in the spring. Pomegranate is one of the few plants that gave its name to a city. The city of Granada in Spain derives its name from this plant.

Schlumbergera Bridgesii
Christmas Cactus

In October and November, when the days shorten to less than twelve hours, the Christmas cactus sets buds. It is not like the desert cactus, loving blazing sun and hot sand. Christmas cactus loves just the opposite: from tropical America, it avoids sun and soil. *Schlumbergera* lives on huge trees, perching in the shade on trunks and branches — yet it does not sap the host. All nourishment is derived from warm, humid air and some occasional dead matter from the tree, on which it holds in position with its wiry legs. (Such a plant is called '*epiphyte*')

The body of Christmas cactus is a chain of glossy green leaflike joints, occasionally branched into a V, and on the tip grow flowers of exquisite form and color. From two- or three inches-long tubes flare petals on three levels, colored in two tones of brilliant pink. The beautiful flowers will form for several months under certain conditions: if night temperature is below 65° F and if uninterrupted darkness is maintained for 12 hours or more. Low-intensity colored lights or moonlight will not affect the forming of buds (same conditions as for flowering of *Poinsettias* and *Chrysanthemums).*

Christmas cactus should be potted in soil with a large amount of peat moss. When buds form, and during the flowering period, the soil should be kept moist, otherwise buds dry up and fall off. After flowering, keep dry. Propagation is very easy: cuttings of two or three joints should be left to dry up for several days and then rooted in moist sand. Cuttings taken in spring will flower the same year. (Four or more in pot make a bushier plant.)

Other *Schlumbergeras* are cultivated. Best known is the "Easter cactus" — *S. gaertneri* — with starlike red flowers, blooming in March and April.

Similar to *Schlumbergeras* is *Zygocactus truncatucs* (see below.)

Tibouchina Semidecandra
Glory Bush

Also called "princess flower," this gorgeous

Schlumbergera bridgesii.

plant has soft, velvety leaves covered with white hair. It grows fairly tall, ultimately—if let so—up to 10 feet high. However, the glory of this plant are large, deep-blue, flowers about three inches in diameter, attracting immediately the attention of visitors. The beautiful blossoms are born from May until January. Good light, but not sun, is necessary for blooming. Soil should be kept moist. Propagation is by cuttings of half-ripened wood taken after the flowering period. *Tibouchina* is the original native name used in Brazil, its land of origin. *Semidecandra* means *half ten stamened.*

Zygocactus Truncatus
Thanksgiving Cactus

Similar in appearance and culture to Christmas cactus, *(Schlumbergera bridgesii*, see above), easy to distinguish by the teeth on its joints. Its flowers are red, with a tendency to grow horizontally. It blooms in November and December.

Other varieties of Thanksgiving cactus have orange-red and salmon flowers.

Special-Effect Plants
for
Solid-Roof Structures

Clusia

Large, thick, and shiny leaves characterize this indoor plant. In its native Panama and Venezuela it grows to the height of 20 feet, but indoors is satisfied with filtered light, warmth, and moist soil. Large, waxy, pink flowers add beauty to *Clusia rosea.*

The *C. rosea aureo-variegata* has dark-green leaves variegated with streaks in light-green and yellow. The common name for this variety is "Monkey apple tree." (*Aureo-variegata* means *variegated with gold. C. grandiflora,* from Quiana, has enormous white and rose flowers 6 to

Zygocactus ***truncatus.***

8 inches across. (*Grandiflora* means *large flowered.)* Propagation is by cuttings of half-ripe wood rooted in sand under cover with bottom heat. It is a good house plant.

Eranthemum Nervosum
Blue Sage

This is a winter-blooming plant with small, blue flowers. The veins of the leaves are prominently depressed, giving the name *nervosum: nerved.* It has to be kept moderately moist. However, if subjected to the excessive moisture in a very humid atmosphere, fungus will start to grow on the leaves. It is generally grown as an annual. Propagation is from cuttings rooted in sand. It is an insect-free, undemanding plant, originating in India. *Eranthemum* in Greek means *lovely flower*.

Eucharis Grandiflora
Amazon Lily

This plant grows in Colombia, South America, from a bulb about 2 inches in diameter. Although the leaves are handsome, glossy from 6 to 12 inches long, the main attraction are large, fragrant, white blossoms. Normally *Eucharis* has to be kept moderately moist. However, if after flowering it is allowed to be dryed off, with sparse watering, and so rested for a few weeks, then again watering well, new flowers will be produced. This can be repeated all year around, if leaves are not lost and bulb is strong and large. When the leaves are let dry, then the bulb must be left alone, until it starts growing again after several months (like *Amarylis*). An insect-free plant, it needs warmth and humidity. The name *eucharis* means *very graceful*. *Grandiflora* means *large flowered*.

Gloxinia (Sinningia Speciosa)

For most people the beautiful plants called Gloxinias, with large, erect, tubular flowers are Gloxinias. Botanical *Gloxinia,* however, is quite a different plant, growing more than two feet tall, branching, with hairy pale-lavender blossoms. (Gloxinia is named after Benjamin Gloxin, German botanist.) The florist Gloxinia is botanically *Sinningia speciosa* (named after William Sinning, a German gardener).

Despite the mix-up of names, the florist Gloxinia is a plant of extraordinary beauty. This beauty came not by a chance; it is a product of intense hybridization. When Gloxinia wakes up in the spring from its dormancy, and spreads thick leaves over the pot, that is only the preparation for the show. Large, tubular flowers rising on thick stems above the leaves arouse everybody. The beautiful trumpets are not limited in color or shape: white, red, rose, blue, purple — spotted or plain; white edged with pink; red with white edges; simple tubes or trumpets filled with ruffles.

To show its beauty properly Gloxinia constantly needs moist soil, and filtered light, yet light of much greater intensity than African violets.

For the show of beauty the Gloxinia prepares a long time. Exhausted from flowering, the plant goes dormant. When it loses its leaves, the watering should be stopped and the pot put into a dry, cool place, preferably a basement. During the active growth fertilizers should be applied to support the flowers and to supply enough nutrients for the tuber to store nourishment for the future show. In the spring, when leaves start to grow again, the pot should be brought into the light and soil kept moist.

Besides the normal-size plants, Gloxinia also grows in miniature size. *Sinningia pusilla (pusilla* means very small) a native to Brazil, has leaves only a half inch in diameter and flowers only three quarters of an inch long. The overall size of the plant is only two inches. The pale blue flowers are produced continually, if the plant is kept in the high humidity of a terrarium or a bowl covered with glass or plastic. If grown in the room air, this tiny plant goes dormant from late fall until January, which is a short dormancy compared to that of large Gloxinias.

Two hybrids of *S. pusilla* are *S.* 'Doll Baby' and *S.* 'Tom Thumb.' Both are small plants. *S.* 'Doll Baby' is about three inches across and has pale lavender flowers one inch long. *S.* 'Tom Thumb' is larger. Flowers are about one-and-half-inch-long trumpets, velvety red with white edge. Both miniatures can be raised as house plants.

Seeds of Gloxinia are readily available and can be started any time of the year. Plants started from seeds will bloom in about seven months. The leaf of a matured Gloxinia will also develop into a plant, but it takes much longer than from the seed.

Hoya carnosa 'Exotica.'

Another way to propagate Gloxinia is by division of the tuber.

Hoya
Wax Plant

A very popular house plant, the *Hoya* comes from the tropics of Asia and Australia. Some of these vines are adaptable to house conditions, others require the light and humidity of a garden room. All have thick, fleshy leaves and small waxy flowers born in clusters. The peculiarity of *hoyas* is the growing of flowers from the same old spurs, year after year. Even if the old spurs are unsightly, they must not be removed. No spurs, no flowers. The flowering time is spring and summer. In winter *Hoyas* should be kept more dry. Because of the thick, waxy leaves, these plants do not require moist soil, but moderately dry, and grow well in filtered light. Propagation is by air layering or by cuttings of year-old wood rooted in sand with bottom heat. It is named after British gardener Thomas Hoy.

H. bella is a dwarf, nonclimbing. It grows first upright, then its branches start to droop. It has white flowers with purple centers. *Bella* means *handsome*.

H. carnosa is the well known "wax plant" with plain green leaves and pinkish-white flowers having maroon centers. Flowers form rounded heads, each containing 40 to 50 small blossoms. The variegated form, *H. carnosa Variegata,* has green leaves blotched with cream, the young leaves with pinkish tint. *Carnosa* means *flesh colored.*

Quite a bloomer is *H. motoskei,* called spotted *Hoya* for its leaves spotted with silver dots.

Variegated leaves also has *H. purpureo-fusca,* called Silver pink, with pinkish-silver blotches on

Sinningia 'Doll Baby.'

leaves. Its leaf stems are red. The name means *purple-brown,* referring to the color of flowers.

Rosa Roulettii
Rosa Chinensis Minima
Miniature Rose

Nobody knows for sure how this miniature rose of Chinese origin found its way into a small mountain village in Switzerland. It is presumed that a soldier brought it from one of his services overseas. For generations it was cultivated in that tiny village, being grown on window sills of every chalet. And there it was rediscovered, again by a soldier, Major Roulett of the Swiss Army during World War I, and named in his honor.*

A small plant, from three to twelve inches high, it bears double rosy flowers with a pale center. The flowers are about an inch and a half across. Miniature leaves are toothed. Like all roses it requires bright light, sun, and moist soil. Overfeeding will force it to grow out of its miniature size. It is reported to bloom year round in the village in Switzerland where it was found. It is understandable why it blooms continually in the high altitude of the Alps. The rarified air absorbs fewer sun rays and consequently more light is available. Such bright light supports continuous blooming of this little gem even if it is located on a window sill. For me, not living in the high altitude of the Alps, it blooms intermittently.

Propagation is by cuttings of ripened wood in sandy peat under cover. This plant is a parent of all miniature roses.

*Based on a story in the book by A. W. Anderson. *How We Got Our Flowers*. Copyright` 1966 by Dover Publications, Inc. Used with permission.

24

Colorful and Variegated Foliage Plants

If blossom is the highest expression of beauty of some plants, others compete for attention with colors of the leaves. Several *Bromeliads* get on fire at blooming time; many plants keep on colors continually. Some shy away from the sun, which would bleach their coloring. On the contrary, others need sun to maintain colorful pigmentation of the leaves.

Not all beauty is in bright coloring. If silver is precious to people and used sparingly, so it is with some plants. Tiny silvery crystals are used in narrow strips, small dots, or blotches. Another group of vigorous growers does not want to give up large areas of chlorophyl. The compromise is then yellow or ivory stripes or patches.

Whatever the expression of beauty, every plant with colorful and variegated foliage will brighten any indoor garden.

Colorful and Variegated Plants For Light-Transmitting Roof Structures

Aechmea

Aechmeas belong to *Bromeliad* family and form a very large group of tree-living plants. Each has a leaf cup for holding water. The name means *point* in allusion to pointed sepals. From a great selection only a few are described.

A. 'Bert' is a hybrid developed by M. B. Foster and named for his son. The leaves have colorful brownish markings on light-yellow leaves.

A. chantinii has silver crossbands on different backgrounds: olive green, light green, or brownish. Several variants are available. It needs bright light and good drainage.

A. fasciata is also available in several variants, one having silver bands on light-green leaves; another with silver bands on maroon. Also one variety has light-gold leaves edged with green stripes. One cultivar has golden-edged stripes enclosing silver-banded green leaves. The large blue and pink flower cluster lasts for many months. *Fasciata* means *broadly banded.*

A. fosteriana is quite different. Its large leaves have blotches in pastel colors of blue, green, and pinkish. Similarly, the blossom is multicolored in subdued red, green, and yellow. It was discovered by Mr. Foster in Brazil.

A. orlandiana's peculiarity is in raised dark bands and sunken light-green portions. When found in Brazil in the blooming stage it reminded Mr. and Mrs. Foster of the colors of the city of Orlando, Florida. Therefore, they requested that it be named in honor of their adopted city.

A. racinae is called Christmas jewels. It flowers in December-January in a combination of Christmas colors. The bright green of the leaves is supplemented by the vivid red of the flowers, having yellow and black tips. It is named for Racine, wife of M. B. Foster. This *Aechmea* was found on their trip to Brazil almost by chance. When waiting for a train at a high altitude station, they utilized several hours by collecting. This is a simple but reliable

Aphelandra squarrosa louisae.

plant. Offshoots taken in the spring bloom by Christmas.

Aphelandra
Zebra Plant

The beautifully veined leaves of *Aphelandra* are quite well known, being frequently sold by florists with already started blossoms. Few people succeed in bringing them into flowering again, because the atmosphere in the house is so much different from that of Central and South America, the homeland of these beauties. Warmth, humidity, and moist soil are what *Aphelandras* demand. Cuttings of half-ripened wood root easily in moist sand under cover. Blooming time is summer and fall — if plants are pot bound.

A. aurantiaca has green leaves with gray areas along the veins and bright orange-red terminal flowers. Hence, the name aurantiaca, which means *orange-red*.

The variety *A. aurantiaca roezlii* also comes from Mexico. It has silvery, twisted leaves. It is named for the Czech discoverer Benedict Roezl.

A. squarrosa Louisae the frequently sold "zebra plant" — has pleasantly green leaves deeply embossed with cream veins. Small flowers form vivid yellow, four-cornered spikes. The graceful spikes are up to 6 inches tall and are long lasting. *Squarrosa* means *with parts spreading*, in reference to flowers spreading from the spike.

Alternanthera

This is a group of small plants with differently colored leaves. They are very undemanding — they do not even want rich soil. Often used as bedding plants, this arrival from Brazil has to be sheared in order to be bushy. The intensity of coloring depends on the intensity of light, the brightest colors being available in full sun. Cuttings root very easily in moist sand. Soil should be moderately moist. It is an insect-free plant.

A. amoena's small 1-inch elliptic leaves are brown-red. Flowers are very small, an off-white color. *Amoena* means *charming*.

A. amoena 'Brilliantissima' has two-inch leaves, pink and red with purplish veins if grown in full sun. In bright light the leaves are coppery-red. The name means *most brilliant*.

A. bettzickiana's one-inch leaves are splashed with pink, red, and yellow.Another variety has leaves of yellow and green.

A. versicolor changes color from red in good light to green-bronze in shade. *Versicolor* means *variously colored*.

Begonias

Begonia 'Argenteo-guttata' is also called "Trout Begonia" for the resemblance of its silver spots to those of a trout. The green leaves are heavily spotted with silver dots; has red underside. Blossoms are white to cream with a pink tint if grown in strong light. An "angel wing" *Begonia,* it is properly called *cane type*. Requires good light and moderately moist soil. Cuttings having at least two nodes root easily in water and, like most of "angel wing" *Begonias,* will bloom during rooting. The name means *silver speckled*.

B. boweri 'Bow Nigra' has star-shaped, dark-green, almost black leaves, with sheen. The vein areas are light green, which carries also to the underside, among deep red. All *boweri* hybrids have bristles on edge, called "eyelashes." Blooms in winter with pink flowers, carried on long stalks. A rhizomatous *Begonia,* needs shade amid moderately moist soil. It propagates best from sections of rhizomes. It is named for Miss Constance Bower from San Diego, California.

B. boweri 'Nigra Marga' is a small plant. The light-green leaves have almost black vein areas. The underside is deep red and green. It blooms in winter with small, white flowers. A rhizomatous, plant, culture and propagation are as for the previous *Begonias*.

Calla lily *Begonias* are a small group of wax *Begonias*. The peculiarity, which gave name to these *semperflorens* types, are the terminal leaves: almost white, little curled, looking like *Calla (Zantedeschia)*. The more mature leaves are green with white splashes. The blossom is present most of the time. It needs cooler temperatures and bright light. It should be kept in a cool corner. Keep soil dry as for all *semperflorens*. Cuttings for propagation must be green leaves or at least half of a leaf green. Rooting should be under cover.

B. fusco-maculata is a hybrid. Its medium-sized green leaves have blotches of chocolate brown, and an underside of red and green. Long, hairy stems let the older leaves droop down. Blooms with pink flowers in winter. A rhizomatous *Begonia*, suitable for copious watering or dry soil. It wants shade, and propagates from rhizome cuttings. The name means *brown spotted.*

B. 'Grey Feather' a hybrid that does not bloom easily. The handsome, gray-green leaves have veins outlined in light green. A fibrous rooted *Begonia* needs good light and moderately moist soil. Cuttings will root in water or sand.

B. goegoensis is named after the city Geogo in Sumatra, where it is native. Bronze-green, rounded leaves have light-green vein areas. It has pink blossoms in winter and needs warmth, shade, humidity, and moist soil. Propagates from rhizome cuttings.

B. listida is a fairly new introduction from Brazil. A small plant with boat-shaped leaves in dark green with a light-green stripe running through the center. The underside is dark red with repeating of the light-green band. It has white flowers in winter. Needs good light, humidity, and moderately moist soil. Cuttings root in sand. The name means *striped.*

B. lubbersii is another plant with boat-shaped leaves from Brazil. The dark-green leaves have silver splashes. The white flowers in summer are quite large for this species. It needs good light, humidity, and moderately moist soil. It is fibrous rooted. Cuttings root best in moist sand. It was not found originally in its habitat near Petropolis in Brazil, but was introduced with a tree fern into the Brussels Botanical Garden, where it started to grow on the tree fern's trunk. *Lubbersii* means *clumsy.*

B. Maphil is another boweri hybrid, with star-like leaves, fresh green, having yellow and brown spots. Blossoms are pink. It makes a nice basket plant. It requires moist soil and some shade, and propagates best from rhizome cuttings.

B. 'Orange-rubra' is an "angel wing" hybrid. Its medium-sized leaves are silver spotted. Blossoms are orange-red as the name itself indicates. Flowers quite often without much care. Some shade and moderately moist soil are the requirements. Cuttings root easily in water or sand.

B. palmaris. Each leaf is a multipointed star of dark green with light-green center, and spreading light-green bands. Edges are light brown with bristles, and its leaves are carried on long, pink stalks. Flowers are pink. It is a rhizomatous *Begonia* from Mexico, wanting shade and moderately dry soil. The name means *like a palm.*

B. 'Pinafore' is a small-growing angel-wing hybrid with bluish-green, silver-spotted leaves and a red underside. Needs some shade and moderately moist soil. The flowers are pink. Cuttings root in water or sand.

B. 'Sophie Cecile' is an angel-wing hybrid with deeply cut, dark-green leaves having large, silver streaks, and a red underside. If well kept, the silver streaks have pink overlay. It has very nice pink blossoms and requires some shade and moderately moist soil. Cuttings root easily in water or sand.

B. mazae is one of the few *Begonias* with fragrant blossoms, imitating the fragrance of tea rose. Blooms in January-February with pink flowers. The leaves are 2 to 3 inches, almost round, having light centers and dark areas along the veins. It needs filtered light and moderately moist soil. This rhizomatous plant propagates easily from a section of rhizome. It is named for Señor Maza, from Mexico, on whose farm it was found.

Billbergias

Billbergias belong to the *Bromeliad* family and are quite similar to the *Aechmeas* in their structure. All have water-holding cups. The large flower clusters generally hang down in contrast to *Aechmeas,* which have erected flower heads (with few exceptions like *A. racinae).* They are named for Swedish botanist Billberg. Propagation is by offshoots.

B. brasiliensis has colorful leaves of broad, silver bands alternating with maroon bands. Large pink sepals and blue petals make it a very beautiful plant.

B. 'Fantasia' is called "rainbow plant," the bronze leaves are splashed with cream and pink. At flowering time the red and blue blossoms bring more rainbow colors.

B. venzuelana has the most attractive flowers of all *Bromeliads.* Quite a tall plant at its three feet, it has copper leaves crossbanded with silver.

Calatheas

These beautiful foliage plants from South America are close relatives of the *Marantas* and

Ctenanthe, and require the same culture. The brilliant, often metallic green of the leaves, is blotched, spotted, and striped in purple, pink, cream, and different shades of green in stunning patterns. To maintain beautiful colors, Calatheas need rich, humusy soil, and monthly fertilizing. Filtered light and moist soil are other requirements. Propagation is by division of matured plants in February-March.

C. makoyana is called "peacock plant" after the design of the leaves resembling the design of peacock feathers. The wide, ovate leaves have designs in lines and ovals in different shades of green and cream. The same pattern is repeated on the reverse side in purple colors.

C. ornata 'Roseo-lineata' has metallic green leaves intersected with narrow, pink stripes. *Ornata* means *ornate. Roseo-lineata* means *pink lined.*

C. veitchiana is very beautiful. The twelve inches long leaves have four different shades of green and a peacock feather design in pale yellow. The same design is repeated in red on the underside of the leaves.

C. zebrina forms large, velvety green leaves with light-green stripes. It is an often-grown plant. *Zebrina* means *zebra striped.*

Chirita Sinensis
Silver Chirita

Chiritas belong to the *gesneriad* family. Most of them live in shade and moist soil along the creeks of India and South East Asia. The beautiful *Chirita sinensis,* which comes from Southern China, grows in dry areas on stony slopes contrary to the other *Chiritas* and most *Gesneriads*. It forms a low rosette of gorgeous, emerald-green leaves, richly inlaid with crystallike silvery areas. The thick and hairy leaves enable *C. sinensis* to survive dry seasons. In cultivation it must be handled accordingly: when in active growth it should be kept moist; otherwise the soil should be dry (during summer). Soil should be sandy. Flowering occurs only in strong light. The purplish flowers add beauty to the plant, which is very beautiful even without them. Propagation is from seeds or leaf cuttings under cover. The name is Hindi, transferred from another plant of the Gentian family. *Sinensis* means *Chinese*.

Cissus Discolor

This beautiful vine has leaves with reddish veins and raised areas between veins overlaid with silver. The young leaves intermix pinkish tint with silver; the underside is maroon. Coming from Southeast Asia, *Cissus* requires warmth, filtered light, and moist soil. During winter the active growth stops and leaves fall off; the long vines then should be cut off. The soil should be watered weekly to prevent the dormant plant from drying out. New growth starts in March. It propagates easily from cuttings in moist sand. It is an excellent climber. *Cissus* is Greek for *ivy. Discolor* means *of two colors*.

Codiaeum–Croton

The botanical name of these beauties is *Codiaeum*. Extensive hybridization has created leaves of different patterns and a great variety of colors. Some look like oak leaves, others are narrow ribbons; the broad and large leaves are contrasted with small and thin ones. The varied form of leaves is surpassed by yet a greater variety of colors: shades of green, red, maroon, pink, yellow, and orange, intermingle in blotches and stripes, creating bizarre formations. Generally, the young leaves are green, the coloring developing as the leaves mature.

The brilliance of colors depends on the brightness of light. Some *Crotons* can take full sun, but the newer hybrids must be protected from direct sun. They can be also raised as house plants, providing they get good light, warmth, moist soil, and not too low humidity. If the light is not sufficient, the leaves turn green.

Florists handle certain hybrids; but the named varieties can be purchased from catalogues. The native land of *Crotons* is tropical Asia.

Propagation is by cuttings in winter, in sandy peat with bottom heat, also by air layering. Leaves of *Crotons* are used for wreaths in their native lands, from which is derived the Greek name *Codiaeum,* meaning *head*.

Coleus

The king of colorful foliage is unquestionably *Coleus*. No other plant puts so boldly intense col-

Coleus blumei Hybrid.

ors side by side in such beautiful combinations. Bright red or pink next to black or vivid green forms unusual leaves. In other combinations the light pink penetrates the vine red, yellow joins red or green, rainbow colors intermix — or just the satin black covers the leaves and lets the green of the underside peak in at the ruffled edges. All these gorgeous color combinations develop in bright light. A deficiency of light also produces a deficiency of colors.

The blossoms, growing in tall spikes, are of blue color and small, almost undesirable, disturbing the bold color combinations. If left on the plant, they soon are generous with tiny seeds, sprouting easily in neighboring pots or beds. Often the flowers are pinched off, as not to disturb the beautiful leaves. Planted in a ground bed, *Coleus* can grow within one year to a height of three to four feet. But its useful lifetime is limited to a maximum of two years. Even by that time it is a woody, straggly plant. Cuttings root very easily in water or sand and can provide enough plants for a shady spot outdoor in summer.

The beauty of *Coleus* is quite fragile, not only because it breaks easily but also because it freezes easily. A temperature slightly above 40°F is fatal. The roots are very shallow, therefore soil must be kept moist to prevent wilting. Few plants can rival the beautiful leaves of this gift from the island of Java.

Hypoestes Sanguinolenta
Pink Polka Dot

One of the few plants you do not have to worry about propagating. After flowering, the seeds scatter and soon you find in nearby pots and flower beds new seedlings growing without your care. The main feature of this plant are small pink dots on dark green leaves. The variety 'Splash' has bigger leaves and the pink dots are enlarged into rosy-pink splashes. This good grower from Madagascar blooms in summer with small, blue flowers. It needs filtered light and moist soil. *Sanguinolenta* means *bloody (splattered with blood).*

Oxalis

Plants of this family grow all over the world (Wood sorrel). Some of the tropical species, suitable for an indoor garden, are dormant either in summer or in winter. These types are often sold by florists. One is called "lucky clover" or "good luck plant" (*Oxalis deppei*) blooming in winter. Another is "Grand duchess *oxalis*" (*Oxalis purpurea*), also blooming in winter, with large, rosy flowers. The "Irish shamrock" (*Trifolium repens*), the white-blooming clover sold for St. Patrick's Day, is not an *Oxalis*, although it looks like one.

A number of tropical *Oxalis* are perennials, having beautiful leaves or flowers, and are active all year. The leaves of many are similar to clover, even if often colored and veined. All want bright light and moderately dry soil. Many propagate from bulbs, or division of rhizomes; some from cuttings. *Oxalis* is a Greek word for *sour*.

O. hedysaroides rubra — 'Fire fern' — from South America, is a beautiful, erect plant with satiny red leaves, resembling the fine-cut foliage of a fern, sensitive to the touch. Its flowers are bright yellow, protruding on long stalks, making a nice color combination. It propagates from cuttings. *Hedysaroides* means *like hedysarum* (an herb of pea family). *Rubra* means *red*.

O. martiana 'auero-reticulata' is a gorgeous, small plant, growing from bulbs and producing cloverlike leaves, beautifully veined in yellow color. Carmine flowers, growing in clusters, rise above the low spreading foliage. The three leaflets fold together for the night and will do the same also during the day if the temperature rises above 80°F or if exposed to direct sunshine. In summer, if subjected to high temperatures, it goes dormant. It is better to move it to some other room with a moderate temperature. When it goes dormant, no watering will stop it. The pot then should be put into a darker place in the garden room and occasionally watered, to prevent complete drying out. In November small leaves start to peak out; the plant should be put back in bright light and kept moderately moist, preferably by bottom watering. Propagation is by division of small bulbs. It is named for Dr. Martius, from Germany, who collected and studied plants of Brazil. *Aureo-reticulata* means *with golden veins*.

O. ortgiesii grows to 18 inches tall with deep-green and brown-red leaves, and a maroon underside. The leaves grow three together and have a fishtail shape. Small, yellow flowers form all year, but open only in sun. It comes from the Andes mountains of Peru, and propagates by division of rhizome. It is named after M. Ortgies, director of botantical gardens in Zurich, Switzerland.

O. siliquosa is a dense, low-growing plant with red stalks and reddish leaves. Yellow flowers appear in spring. It is from Costa Rica and propagates from cuttings. *Siliquosa* means *bearing siliques* (long narrow seed pods).

Oxalis is an insect-free plant.

Pedilanthus Tithymaloides Variegatus
Ribbon Cactus

At first look this plant resembles an artificial one. The dark-green, zigzag-bent stems are undiminished in thickness as they stretch straight up. From each sharp bend grows a leaf: the vivid green, wide band running through the center is enclosed by pinkish cream areas along the edges. If grown in poor light, the edge areas revert to light green. The flowers are bright red with a spur, looking like a slipper.

Unlike most members of the *Poinsettia* family (*Euphorbiaceae*), this one has to be kept moist. If too dry, the lower leaves start to drop off. For good leaf coloration it needs strong light. It is native to the Caribbean and also to Florida. Cuttings root in sand and have to be handled like *Poinsettia* cuttings. *Pedilathus* means *slipper*

Pedilanthus tithymaloides variegatus.

Philodendron hastatum.

flower. *Tithymaloides* means *resembling Tithymalus* (another member of the *Euphorbia family*).

Pellionia

Pellionia is closely related to *Pilleas,* but has more variegated foliage. Being a plant from South-east Asia, it needs filtered light, warmth, humidity, and moist soil. It is easily propagated from cuttings in moist sand.

P. daveauana has bronzy leaves with a beautifully contrasting light-green center. A trailing plant, it is good in a hanging basket.

P. pulchra (means *beautiful)* has light-green leaves interlaced with brown veins, pinkish on the underside, and is also good for a basket. *Pellionia is named for French naval officer Pellion.*

Philodendron

The indispensable house plant! These natives of the tropical Americas mostly cling to the trees, using them as support. Hence the name, which means *tree loving*. From steaming jungles, many adjust to the dry air and soil encountered in house cultivation. Under such conditions *Philodendron* grows slowly, leaves are small, and it very seldom produces blossoms. But the same plant put in the greenhouse or garden room grows rapidly, has large leaves, and blooms yearly.

However, the nicest *Philodendron* do not adapt to the house culture. For production of beautiful foliage they need humid air, filtered light, and an abundance of moisture; even wet feet do not cause harm. The *Philodendrons* worth the garden room space are:

P. andreanum has ivory veins on iridescent, dark-green, oblong leaves; its edges are translucent.

P. hastatum (domesticum) is also a good house plant. In an indoor garden it develops spear-shaped leaves to 18 inches in length with light-green veining and beautiful, fragrant blossoms 6 inches tall. The blossoms start to grow in December and mature in March-April. Blossoms open always about five o'clock in the afternoon and after dark, fill the room with a strong fragrance. The spathe, red inside, enclosing the white spadix, stays open only 24 hours. Before closing it emits again a strong fragrance. We always wait for this unusual yearly performance of the nicest blossom of all *Philodendrons*. *P. hastatum* is a robust grower. An older plant will develop air roots growing to the length of 10 feet. *P. hastatum variegatum* has large areas in light and dark green, yellow and cream. *Hastatum* means *spear shaped*.

P. 'Golden Erubescens' has large, spear-shaped leaves in golden-yellow color, while the underside and the new leaves are pink. *Erubescens* means *blushing*.

P. melanochrysum has black-green large leaves with pinkish tint and pinkish veins. The name means *black gold*.

P. squamiferum has leaves in a very different form. The bright green leaves are divided into five lobes, the center lobe being oblong, others smaller and pointed. Leaf stalks are covered with white or red bristles, hence the name: *having scales*.

P. verrucosum has iridescent, heart-shaped leaves in satin, bronze-green with light-green areas along the veins. The bronzy areas are reddish on the underside. The blossom is a white spadix enclosed in purplish spathe. It is the nicest of *Philodendrons*.

The described plants are climbing types and need some support. Propagation is by terminal cuttings of sections with several leaves rooted in sand, also by air layering.

Piper
Ornamental Pepper

Ornamental peppers belong to the large pepper family, the black pepper being the most important member. This spice commanded extremely high prices and gave to the importing merchants great riches. It was the principal drive behind the efforts to open sea routes to India and also the cause of the discovery of America. A common and plentiful product of today, it is without much interest. More interesting are other members of this family, attracting with beautiful variegation of leaves.

P. magnificum is an erect plant from Peru. The oval, shining, green leaves are graced with creamy veins and edges; the underside is red. *Magnificum* means *magnificent*.

P. ornatum is a vine having broad leaves of brocade appearance in dark-green color interwo-

Sanchezia nobilis.

ven with pinkish, which changes in older leaves into a white color. It comes from Celebes. *Ornatum* means *ornate*.

P. sylvaticum an ornamental climber from Burma with thick, dark-green leaves painted silver on raised areas. *Sylvaticum* means *forest loving*.

All pipers need warmth, humidity, filtered light, and moist soil. Cuttings of half-ripe wood root in sand under cover with bottom heat.

Sanchezia Nobilis Glaucophylla

This plant lives up to its name, *nobilis*—noble. It is tall growing, to five feet, with large, lance-shaped leaves prominently painted with yellow veins; the stalk is reddish. Flowers are orange-yellow, appearing in spring-summer and again in winter. It requires warmth, humidity, filtered light, and moist soil. Cuttings of young leaves root in sand under cover. It is an excellent plant from Ecuador. It is named for a Spanish professor, Sanchez. *Glaucophylla* means *glaucous (sea-green) leaved*.

Setcreasea Purpurea

Setcreasea lives up to its name *purpurea (purple)* only when grown in strong light or sun. Otherwise the narrow leaves are gray-green with a slight purplish tint. The best color is obtained in summer, especially if the plant is grown in full sun outdoors. The three-petaled flowers are of lavender color and last only one day. New ones appear daily. It likes plenty of water, although it can survive on meager watering. Cuttings root easily in moist sand.

Strobilanthes Dyerianus

This beautiful foliage plant from Burma has nar-

Strobilanthes dyerianus.

row, pointed, several-inch-long leaves that are iridescent purple, with silver underlay. The veins and edges are green; the underside is maroon. It is fast growing, but does not branch easily. The older plants are somewhat straggly. Yet *Strobilanthes* makes it up with an ease of propagation: cuttings of any size have healthy roots within two weeks. In this manner it is possible always to have a profusion of beautiful plants, which greatly add to the decor.

Flowers are another peculiarity. They grow from a leaf axis on independent, erect spikes two to fourteen inches tall, accompanied with tiny, silver-spotted leaves. The deep-blue, cone-shaped blossoms are about one inch long. The leaves go through several color stages: older leaves become more silvery; dying leaves turn golden-yellow.

Strobilanthes needs warmth, good, filtered light, humidity, and constantly moist soil. It grows well even if the pot stands in a shallow bowl of water. Propagation is from cuttings of young wood in sandy peat, under cover, with bottom heat. It will also root in water in a vase on the kitchen table.

Very similar is *S. Exotica,* a species from New Guinea, having narrower leaves and a slightly carmine color.

Strobilanthes means *cone flower*. *Dyerianus* is named in honor of Sir W. Dyer, British botanist.

Tillandsia

These members of the *Bromeliad* family need very little attention. The scales covering the leaves can extract moisture directly from the air. The name is explained in the introduction to *Bromeliads*. It can be grown easily in a pot or wired to a piece of wood or branch. If the atmosphere is humid enough, no extra attention is necessary, although occasional misting is beneficial.

T. lindenii forms a rosette about 15 inches across. The leaves are marked with maroon bands. The beautiful flower spike, standing high above, is pink and has blue flowers, lasting many weeks. It needs more warmth, moisture, and humidity than other *Bromeliads*. It is named for Jean Linden, Belgian plant collector.

T. cyanea is a small rosette formed by green, narrow leaves, only a half inch wide. At flowering time a large spike rises from the center. The pink colored spike, 8 inches tall and 3 inches wide, looks enormous next to the narrow leaves. On the edges of the spike grow deep-blue flowers. The name *cyanea* means *blue*.

T. usneoides (Spanish moss), is a nice, free souvenir to bring home from a visit to the South, where it grows on trees or even on telephone wires. In the garden room it can cover a bare spot high at the roof. It will not grow as much as it does in nature, but it will prosper. The name means *Like an usnea* (a form of lichen).

Xanthosoma Lindenii

Some *Xanthosomas* are raised in the tropical Americas for edible tubers, similar to the sweet potato. The ornamental *X. lindenii* has large, arrowhead leaves in bright green intersected with yellowish veins. In the variety *Magnificum* the cream areas along the veins are larger amd more pronounced. Warm and humid atmosphere, filtered light, and moist soil are the requirement of this highly ornamental plant. Propagation is by division of the rootstock or by offshoots from the base of the plant. *Xanthosoma* is the Greek name for *yellow stigma*. *Lindenii* is named for the famous Belgian plant collector Jean Linden.

Colorful and Variegated Plants For Solid-roof Structures

Aechmeas

Aechmea 'Foster's Favorite' is a hybrid having smooth, glossy, wine-red leaves. The mutant of this plant, called *Favorite,* retains the wine-red coloring but has yellow stripes on the edges. This mutant, *A. 'Foster's Favorite Favorite,'* is quite an expensive plant.

A. fulgens discolor needs low-intensity light for developing good coloring. The gray-green leaves have a purple underside and are covered with white powder. The blossom is a bright-red-cluster. *Fulgens* means *shining*. *Discolor* means *of two colors*.

A. marmorata is called "Grecian vase" for its tall, tubular shape. Gray-green leaves are splashed with dark green and purple—hence the name, which means *marbled*. Flowers are pink and blue.

A. 'Royal Wine' is a hybrid. Its dark-green leaves are wine-red on the underside. The red flowers, forming large clusters, have blue petals.

Aechmeas propagate from offshoots and belong to the Bromeliad family.

Aglaonema

Although from tropical Asia, *Aglaonemas* are excellent house plants. Easily adapting to low light levels, these very undemanding plants are slow growing. They can be kept on the dry side — or grown directly in water. The blossom is a small white spadix enclosed in green spathe, pollinating itself easily if the plant is moved or shaken. The fruits are small berries, yellow, red, or orange. Each berry contains one seed, which should be sown when fresh. It can also be propagated by divison of older plants or by cuttings rooted in sand or water.

A. commutatum elegans has dark-green leaves with silvery-gray feather design. It blooms as a small plant and is very undemanding. *Commutatum* means *changing*.

A. commutatum 'White Rajah' (Pseudobracteatum) has oblong leaves of pleasant green that are heavily spotted and blotched in cream color, which changes in older leaves into gray-green. This beautiful plant needs warmth.

A. costatum is low and very slow growing. The dark-green leaves have a strong, white streak through the center, accompanied by white spots. *Costatum* means *ribbed*.

A. crispum is often called *Schismatoglottis roebelinii*. This large plant with long leaves has a gray-green design. *Crispum* means *quivering*.

Aglaonemas are insect-free plants.

Alocasia

These large-leaved plants from tropical Asia

Aglaonema commutatum 'White Rajah.'

Alocasia 'Amazonica.'

come from territories like Burma, Borneo, Ceylon, and Sumatra; they need a warm and humid atmosphere. The lowest temperature at night should not be less than 60° F. The soil should be rich and light with a generous amount of peat moss; they can be be grown also in pure peat or sphagnum moss. In that case, they have to be fertilized at least once a month. Growing from tubers, *Alocasias* can be propagated from a section of tuber or from the offshoots growing from baby tubers, which have to be carefully separated from the main tuber. The growing medium should be kept moist, except during the winter months, when these beautiful foliage plants rest somewhat.

A. amazonica does not have anything in common with the Amazon river. It is a hybrid with shiny, dark-green leaves having strong lines of white ribs.

A. cuprea is quite small. The leaves are almost oval, dark metallic green, and corrugated; the underside is purple. *Cuprea* means *copper colored.*

A. sanderiana has deeply scalloped leaves over 12 inches long in silver-green color. The ribs are wide, off-white, stark lines; the underside is purple.

A. watsoniana is called "the queen of alocasias." The large and wide leaves are richly veined in silvery color on bluish-green background with a purple underside. It is named in honor of British botanist E. Watson.

Begonias

Begonia cathayana is from China and carries the old name used for China—Cathay. The beautiful, tapered, dark-green leaves of velvet quality have a zone of light green outlining the shape of the leaf. The red underside has a similar green band. It has yellow flowers in hot summer. Quite touchy but worth trying. Needs humidity, warmth, and dry soil. Overwatering will kill it. Propagation is from seeds or stem cuttings under cover, if possible with bottom heat.

B. 'Emerald Jewel' is a beautiful hybrid having large areas along the veins alternated with emerald-green splashes. Needs shade and dry soil; it is best to water it from below. The greenish-white flowers in winter are insignificant. It is rhizomatous, and is propagated from rhizome or a leaf cutting.

B. imperialis displays imperial colors of bronze-green leaves with smaragd green along the veins. This beautiful plant is from Mexico and has small white flowers in winter. It wants warmth, humidity, shade, and moist soil. It is rhizomatous and propagates from rhizome or leaf cuttings. It is a terrarium plant.

B. imperialis smaragdina also is suitable for a terrarium. This small, rhizomatous plant has leaves all of one color—beautiful smaragd, sunken veins in light green. Culture is the same as for *B. imperialis.*

B. masoniana ("Iron Cross") from Southeast Asia is named for its discoverer, Mason. Light-green, puckered leaves carry a brown-black pattern in the center in which many people see the design of the German war decoration, the Iron Cross, hence, the nickname of this *Begonia.* It has insignificant greenish flowers in winter. It is rhizomatous and propagates best from leaf sections, since the rhizome is quite small. Needs good shade. In strong light the center design fades: high humidity and dry soil are required. Best watering is from below.

B. rajah is an exquisite plant from Malaya—small, rhizomatous, and suitable for a terrarium. Its leaves are almost round with raised portions between the veins in reddish-brown, and the vein areas are light green. The underside is red, with vein ribbons in green. The satin sheen adds beauty to the unusual leaves. It has small, pink flowers in winter. It propagates best from leaf cuttings. Seeds take up to four months to germinate. Needs shade, high humidity, and moist soil and does best in a terrarium.

B. rex created a sensation when discovered in 1856. Actually it was not discovered in a rainforest; it was found in London, England, growing with an orchid brought from Assam. For a long time it commanded extremely high prices. The first ones were sold for the equivalent of seven years' wages of a contemporary skilled worker. From the beginning *Rexes* were intensively hybridized, and now parentage is almost impossible to follow. They are seldom of one color; two, three, or four colors form bands, splashes, ribbons, dots, or intermingle, many with a metallic sheen—like silver shining through a thin layer of color. Mostly they are finicky plants, shy of sun, even of bright light, wanting warmth, high humidity, and moist

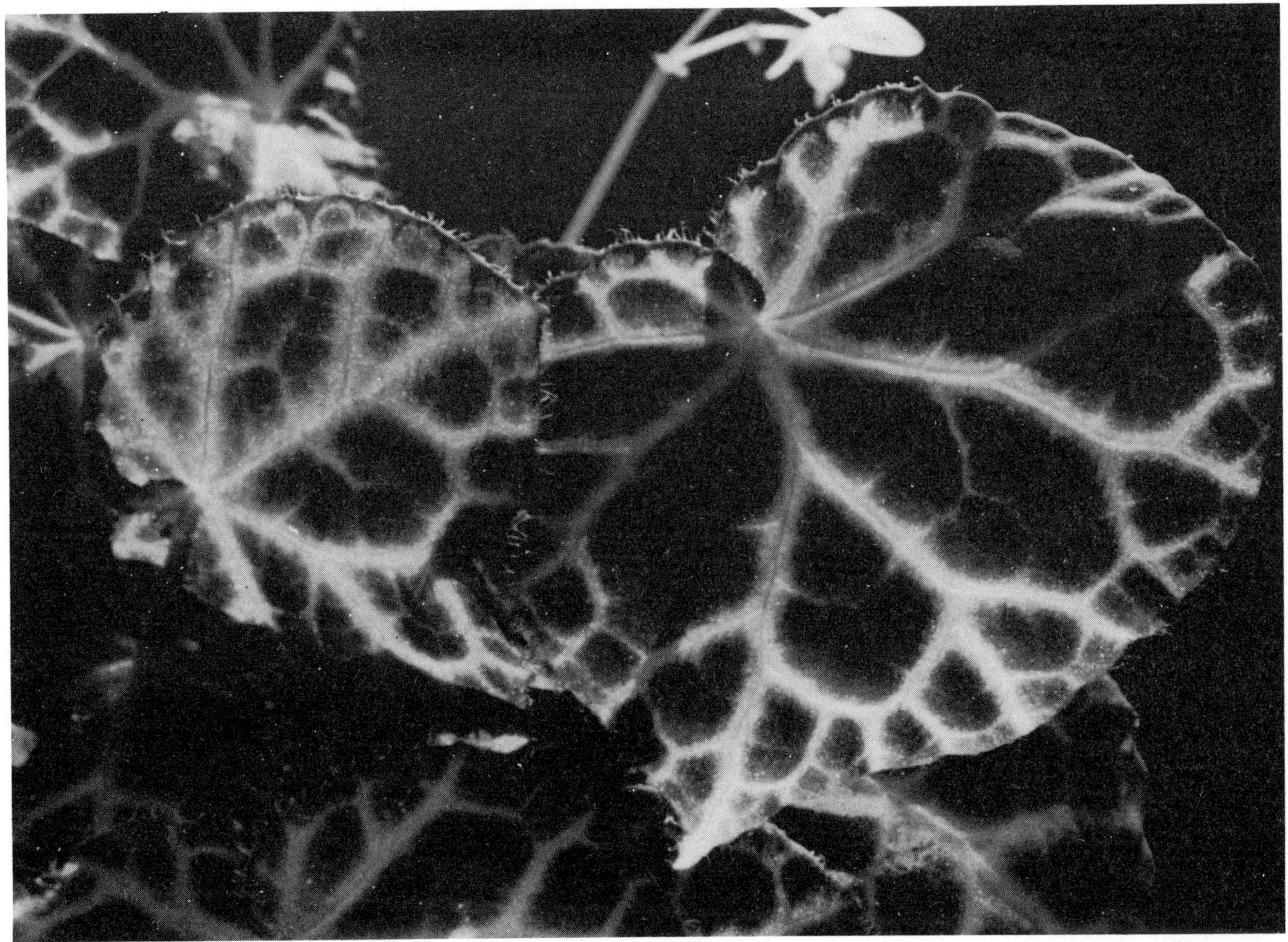

Begonia rajah.

soil. In summer they should be kept in good shade; in winter they should be brought out to the light in order to keep bright coloring. But some are easy to maintain. *Rex Begonias* today are inexpensive, thanks to intense propagation.

B. rex 'Glory of St. Albans' is a British hybrid, one of the most beautiful *Rexes*. Bright silver shines through rosy overlay and brown veins; along the edges is a broad maroon band with rose spots; the underside is dark red. Shy of summer light, it is not the easiest plant to grow, but it is worthy of care and trying. It is an irony that this beauty originated as a chance seedling. It is named for the city of St. Albans in England.

B. rex 'King Edward IV' is a robust grower (for a rex), producing large leaves with dark-brown and green areas, enlivened with silver and red spots. It does not require much care and can be grown as a house plant. However, if cultivated in poor light, the red spots and brown areas recede being replaced by silver and green colors. Even in such coloring it is a very nice plant.

B. rex 'Merry Christmas' is really colorful. The maroon center is encircled in bands of three color: metallic pink, taffeta green with white and pink spots, and maroon. The underside is red and green.

B. rex 'Peace' has a red center and red areas along the veins on a silvery pink field. It is a good grower.

B. rex 'Salamander' is predominantly green with silver blotches in a nice pattern; the underside is red. It is of an easy culture.

Rex Begonias have small pinkish flowers that are insignificant next to the colorful foliage. Best propagation is by leaf sections; also by sections of

Begonia rex 'Merry Christmas.'

rhizome. The name *rex* means *king*. It was given by chance. When a prominent grower saw the first *rex Begonia,* he exclaimed: "A King's *Begonia.*"

B. pustulata argentea is a small, spreading plant having silver areas on light-green leaves. The flowers are greenish. It requires shade, warmth, humidity, and moist soil. It is rhizomatous and propagates from sections of rhizome.

B. versicolor is a small plant from China. Its almost round leaves have areas along veins in dark green, enclosing silver green strips, appearing to radiate from the center. It is covered with red hair, especially prominent on the young leaves, and forms reddish fringe on all leaves. Pink blossoms are frequent, mainly if *B. versicolor* is kept in a terrarium. It is rhizomatous. *Versicolor* means *variously colored.*

Callisia

Callisia is a small group of vining or hanging plants, similar to *Tradescantias,* with very fragrant flowers. All need warmth, humidity, filtered light, amd moist soil. Cuttings root easily in water or sand.

C. elegans (called also *Setcreasea stratiata)* is from Mexico. Its dark-green leaves are elegantly striped lengthwise with white; it has a purple underside. Its flowers are small and white.

C. fragrans (meaning fragrant) lives up to its name: clusters of white flowers emit a fragrance similar to that of *Hyacinth.* The narrow leaves, about 12 inches long, form rosettes. The variety *Melnikoff* has leaves striped white and retains the fragrant flowers.

Sometimes these plants are listed as *Sprionema.*

Ceropegia Woodii
Rosary Vine; Heart Vine

This small vine from East Africa forms long, wiry strings with pairs of heart-shaped, small, green leaves blotched in silver-gray. The underside of the leaves and the thin, wiry stems are purplish. The waxy flowers are pinkish, always, in pairs and looking like small lanterns. On the veins grow small bulbils, which gave it also one common name: rosary vine. The bulbils can be used for propagation and planted. It is also propagated by cuttings rooted in sand. This very good house plant requires partial shade, warmth, and dry soil. *Ceropegia* means *wax fountain,* an allusion to the waxy flowers.

Chlorophytum
Spider Plant

A well-known and cultivated house plant, *Chlorophytum* is satisfied with poor light, bad location, and neglect — although it should be kept moist. The narrow, green leaves arch gracefully, forming a rosette. Before flowering time, from the center of the rosette starts to grow a long runner on which later appear white, starlike blossoms. After the flowering, at the end of the runner develops a new rosette of leaves. This feature — spreading leaves, hanging in midair on a thin runner like a spider—is the origin of the popular name of the *Chlorophytum*. The hanging rosette, when developed, can be cut off and potted—a fast way to a new plant.

The green leaf *Chlorophytum* is called *comosum* (which means *with long hair).* The variety *C. comosum Variegatum* has longer leaves with cream stripes. *Chlorophytum* means simply *green plant*. It is an insect-free plant.

Cryptanthus

The strange-sounding name translated from Greek means *hidden flower*. These *Bromeliads* have little flowers hidden in the small center of the plant. Narrow, pointed leaves form a flat rosette and grow in the soil. M.B. Foster called them affectionately "earth stars." They are very easily propagated, since they grow after flowering a number of offshoots. Some are very colorful.

C. bromelioides tricolor has leaves striped in green, cream and pink. The amount of pink color depends on good light. It is a very beautiful plant.

C. fosterianus has leaves 2 inches wide, dark brown with zigzag silver markings.

C. hybrid 'It' forms leaves up to 18 inches with stripes of orange-pink and cream on reddish-brown or purple background. The underside of the leaves is silvery.

C. zonatus comes in several variations. All have narrow, silver markings on green or brown leaves.

Cryptanthus should be kept moderately dry.

Dieffenbachia
Dumb Cane Plant

The common name is a reminder of the use of the juices of *Dieffenbachia* by natives in the South American tropics to induce 24-hours speechlessness. The large, ornamental leaves are blotched and streaked in shades of green, cream, and white. As the plant grows taller, the lower leaves drop off and the thick cane holds a tassel of leaves at the top. If too unsightly, the top can be cut off and potted directly in the soil, starting a new plant. The thick cane can be cut into sections about two inches long, each having at least one "eye"; the ends should be dusted with sulphur. When put lengthwise, halfway into the sand or soil and kept moist, a new plant will sprout from the eye. With such an ease of propagation *Dieffenbachia* makes up for the lack of perfect form. Some older plants, especially the robust *D. gigantea* (which means *gigantic,)* bloom even when grown in the house. The blossom is similar to that of *Philodendron,* having a green spathe enclosing a white spadix. Actually *Dieffenbachia* grows faster in the house, where the temperature does not fall below 65° F, than in an indoor garden with the night temperature kept at 60° F.

This is a widely cultivated plant and many varieties are on the market. *Dieffenbachias* like moderately dry soil and warmth. Light is not a very important factor. It is named for German botanist Dieffenbach.

Dracaena

Sometimes mistaken for palms, *Dracaenas* are durable indoor plants. To this group also belongs the legendary "dragon tree" of the Canary Islands, known to the ancient Greeks, which gave the name to these plants (*Dracaena* in Greek means *female dragon).* Although relatives of the "Hawaiian Ti plant" *(Cordyline terminalis),* they have differently shaped leaves: from a half inch in one to four inches wide in another. Warmth and filtered light are their preference. In watering they have great latitude. I have had one *Dracaena marginata* for three years on wick watering; another from the same species is watered only once a week — and both are growing well. Propagation is by air layering or rooting of stem sections, like *Dieffenbachia*. Most *Dracaenas* are from Africa.

D. deremensis 'Warneckei' has long, over one-inch-wide leaves striped with creamy bands. It grows quite compactly.

D. godseffiana is called 'Gold dust *dracaena.'* A small, freely branching plant, its leaves are only 3 inches long, oval, covered with creamy spots and blotches. This coloring is rich especially in the variety *'Florida Beauty.'*

D. goldieana is a very beautiful plant from Central Africa. The leaves are wide and stubby, having alternate bands of yellow and green. It needs moist soil and humidity in addition to filtered light. Not for house culture, it has to be kept in a garden room.

D. marginata (also known as *D. gracilis)* has very narrow green leaves edged with red ribbons. The lower leaves always drop off and the head — resembling palm is held high above on the slender trunk. *Marginata* means *margined; gracilis* means *slender*.

D. sanderiana is a small plant. The leaves are elegantly twisted, forming a crown on a short stem. The green center of the leaf is enclosed by two creamy bands.

All *Dracaenas* grow slowly.

Ferns

Several *Pteris* ferns have variegated fronds. See Ferns under "Foliage Plant for Solid-roof Structures."

Fittonia

This small group of small plants is low growing, just hugging the pot and spreading over, with beautifully veined, thin leaves in light green. *Fittonia verschaffeltii* has red veins; *F. argyroneura* (means *silver nerved)* has white veins; *F. pearcei* supplies pink veins.

Fittonias are native to Peru and are of easy culture, blooming even on a window sill with small, pale yellow flowers on spikes. However, the blossom is not the chief attraction—it is only the proof of the modest requirements these plants have. Abundant moisture is necessary for good growth. The best watering is from below, since *Fittonias* do not mind if the saucer or bowl under the pot is full of water for several days. They will not rot, but will grow more luxuriantly. Cuttings root easily in water, soil, or sand. They are named for botanical writers Elizabeth and Sarah Fitton.

Gynura
Velvet Plant

Gynuras are ornamental plants from the Indonesian Islands. Although from the tropics near the Equator, they can adjust to low humidity and light levels of a house, but require moist soil.

G. aurantiaca is an upright, growing with green, fleshy leaves covered with purple hair. It does not branch and has to be pinched for bushy growth. Flowers are orange disks, therefore the name *aurantiaca,* which means *orange-red.*

G. sarmentosa (bicolor) has deeply cut, metallic-green leaves covered with purple hair; it is a nicer looking plant. Forms fast-growing, pendant runners bearing clusters of orange flowers, which give off an unpleasant odor; it is better to cut the flowers off. *Sarmentosa* means bearing runners. *Bicolor* means of two colors. Cuttings root easily in sand.

Hoffmannia
Taffeta Plant

Beautiful creamy or pink veins on silky leaves are the chief attraction of *Hoffmannias,* more so because the leaves are in shades of green and bronze, accordion-folded between veins. Tropical Mexico is the home of these beauties, which require warmth, humidity, shade, and moist soil. They are not easy to grow well. Propagation is by cuttings in sandy peat with bottom heat. They are named after German botanist Hoffmann.

H. ghiesbreghtii has silvery-green leaves intersected with pink veins and a deep-rose underside. The variety *'Variegata'* has blotches of pink, green, brown, and cream. It has small yellow flowers. It is named for Belgian plant collector Ghiesbreght.

H. roezlii has puckered leaves, red in the center; a satin sheen reflects the light; the underside is purple. Small flowers are dark red. Named for Czech explorer Roezl, who was collecting plants in the tropical Americas.

H. vittata is a small plant. The accordion folds are between pale green veins of bronze-green leaves of satin sheen. The young leaves are more bronze. *Vittata* means *striped. Hoffmannias* are sensitive to cold drafts.

Iresine
Blood Leaf

Iresine is an excellent ornamental plant from Brazil. In South America it is used lavishly in gardens, growing to the height of several feet.

I. herbstii has small, almost round leaves of deep-red color with light-red veins. The variety *I. herbstii 'Aureo-reticulata'* (which means *golden veined)* has yellow veins on light green leaves. If grown in strong light, it develops pink blotches.

I. herbstii 'Acuminata' has pointed leaves about 3 inches long, deep red with pink veins. The stems are also red.

Iresine likes moist soil and bright light, but does well as a house plant. Cuttings root easily in water or sand. Flowers are very seldom produced under cultivation, but the whitish, woolly blossoms gave the name to this plant. *Iresine* means in Greek *woolly* garland. It is an insect-free plant.

Maranta
Prayer Plant

The beautiful foliage plants from South America are known for the habit of lifting and closing their leaves for the night. Some adapt to house condi-

Maranta erythroneura.

tions, making good house plants, and are sold frequently by florists. The ones with the most colorful designs need the humidity and filtered light of the garden room. Although in need of moist soil, they rest in winter from December to February, and should be kept dry in that time. *Marantas* bloom several times a year even as house plants with small, pale blue flowers, which are insignificant next to the colorful foliage. Propagation is by division of clumps of older plants done at the time of rest in February. They are named for Italian botanist Maranta.

M. erythroneura is a plant of beautiful coloring. Three shades of green are intersected with gracefully curved red veins. The light-green color forms a bizarre pattern; it has a dark-red underside. It is a good house plant. It keeps coloring even in poor light. *Erythroneura* means *red veined.*

M. leuconeura kerchoveana is the well-known "prayer plant" and is widely sold. The grayish-green, oval leaves have chocolate areas on both sides of the main vein. The intensity of coloring depends on the intensity of light. *Leuconeura* means *white veined.*

M. leuconeura massangeana has a design of leaves almost identical to the *M. erythoroneura,* except in different colors. The gracefully curved veins are white and the dark-green color is bluish. This plant needs the filtered light and humidity of a garden room to grow well and to maintain coloring.

Neoregelia

At flowering time the center of the *Neoregelias* turns brilliant red and the vivid coloring stays for

Neoregelia carolinae 'Tricolor.'

many months after the last blossom fades. It is an invitation to humming birds and insects to visit the flowers and help in pollination. Small flowers are almost hidden in the leaf-cup holding water and would be bypassed by pollinating insects if it were not attracted by the vivid color. In this respect *Neoregelias* and also *Nidulariums* act like *Poinsettia*.

Neoregelias belong to the *Bromeliad* family and are good house plants — but must have sufficient light. The leaf cup has to be filled with water. The name is of mixed origin.

N. carolinae 'Tricolor' forms a spreading rosette of glossy leaves with ivory stripes, which in good light are tinted pink. The center of the rosette keeps the brilliant red color after flowering for more than half a year. It is a good house plant. It is named for Caroline Morren, wife of the editor of a Belgian horticultural magazine.

N. marmorata is a robust plant growing vigorously without much care. The leaves are blotched with maroon, like marble, hence the name *marbled*. The tips of the leaves are painted red. For this feature it is called "fingernail plant." The best coloring is achieved in strong light.

N. spectabilis is another good house plant with the painted fingernails feature. The leaves are metallic green with gray crossbands on underside.

Neoregelias propagate from offshoots.

Nidularium

The name means *nest* as an explanation for almost hidden flowers nested in the center cup. *Nidulariums* are *Bromeliads* living on the floor of the jungle. Pollinating insects and hummingbirds are attracted to hidden flowers by the intense red color, lasting for the flowering period. *Nidulariums* need more moisture than other *Bromeliads* and grow well in peat moss. Propagation is from offshoots formed after flowering.

N. fulgens forms a low rosette of bright-green leaves mottled with dark green. The edges have little spines. It is a very durable house plant. *Fulgens* means *shining*.

N. innocentii is available in several varieties. The prettiest is the variety 'Stratiatum,' with yellow stripes and bands on the green leaves. Named for Mt. St. Innocentii in South Brazil.

Osmanthus Illicifolius Variegatus
Variegated False Holly

The leaves are—as the name *illicifolius* says—like holly: thick, shiny, with spines and with white areas along the edges. The flowers are white and fragrant, appearing in summer. A very decorative, although slow-growing plant, needs good light and quite dry soil. It can be grown in a cooler location. Cuttings of half ripened wood, taken after flowering, root in sand under cover. *Osmanthus* means *fragrant flower*. It is newly called *O. heterophyllus 'Variegatus' (heterophyllus* means *various leaved)*.

Pandanus
Screw pine

Another interesting example of how a large tropical tree can become an excellent house plant. *Pandanus,* growing to a height of 60 feet with leaves 17 feet long, a utility tree of tropical Malaysia and Polynesia: the fruit is food, leaves roofing material, and trunks furnish wood for building huts. Sitting high above ground on stilt roots — it is hard to imagine its young version inside a house.

In cultivation, *Pandanus* develops almost from the pot a rosette of gracefully arching, long and narrow leaves with spines. Only older specimens grow the trunk and stilt roots. Leaves have yellow stripes in *P. sanderii* and white stripes in *P. veitchii*. To maintain stripes on variegated *Pandanus,* the roots must always be moist, otherwise leaves will turn green. Filtered light is satisfactory. Propagation is by offshoots growing from the base. The name *Pandanus* is an adaptation of the native name for screw pine.

Peperomia

The well-known "watermelon *Begonia*" is a *Peperomia (sandersii)*. Several *Peperomias* have been cultivated for a long time as excellent subjects for dish gardens and house plants. Although they come from the hot, steaming rainforests of the tropical Americas, many *Peperomias* adapt to home conditions. A warm house and low-light levels are sufficient for their growth. They do not even need much moisture, but should be kept dry,

Peperomia caperata 'Emerald Ripple.'

Aphelandra squarrosa louisae

Sanchezia nobilis

Peperomia caperata 'Emerald Ripple'

Zebrina pendula 'Quadricolor'

storing water in thick leaves. All are small plants. The cuttings, even leaf cuttings, root easily in moist sand, bottom heat hastening the process. The name means *like pepper* since commercial black pepper belongs to the same family.

From a large number available, the most handsome are:

P. caperata 'Emerald Riple.' The deep corrugations in the dark green leaves gave the name to this cultivar, which raises each leaf on a long stalk, forming a bushy plant. It blooms in spring with erect, tall catkins in greenish color.

P. caperata 'Tricolor' is broadly margined with cream coloring and red around the base.

P. marmorata 'Silver Heart' has heart-shaped leaves with silver strips between light green veins. *Marmorata* means *marbled.*

P. obtusifolia is also called "baby rubber plant." It is an excellent house plant, much cultivated. The dark-green, thick, round leaves are very shiny. Self-branching, it has to be kept quite dry. The variety *Variegata* has wide areas along its pale yellow edges. The name *obtusifolia* means *obtuse leaved.*

P. sandersii shiny leaves are dished, and dark-green bands radiating from the center are alternated with silvery streaks. A well known and much grown plant.

P. verschaffeltii's bluish-green leaves are painted with silver bands between pale yellow veins. This one is not a house plant, requiring high humidity and more filtered light. Peperomias are insect-free plants.

Pilea

The best-known plant from this group is the "artillery plant" — *Pilea microphylla* — for its habit of discharging dry pollen in small puffs. Because it is an annual, cuttings must be taken in time to have new plants.

Another well-known is *Pilea cardierei*, called "aluminum plant," native to Vietnam. Its dark leaves have silver overlay on raised areas. It is also known under the name "watermelon pilea." A smaller version, *P. cadierei Minima,'* has leaves about an inch and a half long; it is slow growing.

The "Pan-American friendship plant" *(Panamiga)* has deep-green or bronze-colored leaves, depending on light intensity. Botanically, *P. involucrata* means *with an involucre,* referring to the chains of minute, greenish flowers growing from the base of the leaves and spreading over them. It is from Peru.

P. 'Silver Tree' is a branching small plant with toothed leaves having a wide silver band running through the center and accompanied by silver spots. It comes from the Caribbean.

Pileas are good house plants requiring filtered light and moist soil. Cuttings root easily in sand. The name means *cap,* as a reference to the flowers.

Pittosporum Tobira Variegatum
Australian Laurel

Not from Australia, although many members of its family grow into trees on that continent, this plant is native to China and Japan. It is a nice, woody, very slow-growing bush with gray-green leaves variegated along the edges in cream. The foliage, when crushed, has a lemon scent. The fragrant flowers, growing in cluster, are similar to orange blossoms. It is a very good plant, needing little care. It needs filtered light and dry soil and does not mind a cool location. Cuttings of half-ripened wood root in sand. The name *Pittosporum* means *sticky seed. Tobira* is a common Japanese name for this plant.

Plectranthus

This group of small-leaved, trailing plants, adapting well to house conditions needs filtered light and moist soil. Cuttings root easily in most sand.

P. australis (parviflorus), from Australia and the Pacific Islands, is called "Swedish ivy." The green leaves are grayish on the underside with purple veins. Small white flowers grow in spikes.

P. coleoides Marginatus is called "candle plant." The name *coleoides* means *resembling Coleus.* The bright-green, *Coleus*like leaves have white areas along the edges. It is a nice trailing plant.

P. oertendahlii is from Natal in East Africa. The small, dark-green leaves have a fine network of white veins and purple edges. The older leaves turn purple underneath as the silver veining fades. Stems are reddish. Small, white flowers grow on erect spikes.

Polyscias Balfouriana Pennockii
White Aralia

Aralias are quite well-known house plants. The botanical name *polyscias* means *many in shade,* referring to the abundant foliage produced in the shade. Coming from the tropics of Asia and Pacific Islands, they require shade and moderately moist soil. Propagation is by tip or joint cuttings rooted in sand. Aralias are mostly foliage plants. The cultivar *Pennockii* has large, waxy leaves in bright green, variegated along the veins in cream color. In strong light the cream areas grow larger.

Rhoeo Discolor
Moses in the Cradle

Rhoeo is a well-known and grown house plant, newly listed as *R. spathacea*. Long, narrow leaves form a rosette of dark-green leaves with purple edges as well as purple underside. The small, white flowers are pushed from a boat-shaped enclosure, nested between the leaves. Each three-petaled white flower lasts only one day, to be followed by another one. The variety *R. spathacea Vittata'* (which means *striped)* has yellow stripes on the green side of the leaves. This form needs more warmth and humidity.

Rhoeo is an undemanding plant, doing well in any corner where there is filtered light, and it wants moderately moist soil. A native of Mexico, it propagates easily from side shoots rooted in sand or from seeds. It even seeds itself. Once I found several seedlings growing in a pot of an old *Rhoeo*. They were unexpected but welcome. *Discolor* means *of two colors*. The origin of the name *Rhoeo* is unknown.

Sansevieria
Snake Plant

A well-known house plant, *Sansevieria* takes much abuse and grows in any location, even in poor light. The thick, succulent leaves are water-holding reservoirs. This implies that *Sansevierias* must be kept dry. Watering once a week is sufficient. They grow from thick rooting stock and spread themselves easily wherever planted: They will fill a pot with new shoots or spread on a large area if planted in ground beds. When a leaf is broken or cut off it will make a nice ornament for many months without shrinking or changing color.

From a large number of *Sansevierias* only few are grown.

S. Trifasciata has narrow stiff leaves growing erect to 4 feet in height (if planted in a ground bed). The zigzag crossbands in dark green resemble design patterns found in some *Bromeliads*. This is the plant called "mother-in-law's tongue." In juvenile form it is often planted in dish gardens. It comes from East Africa and propagates from offshoots, also from 3 inches long sections of leaf inserted into moist sand. *Trifasciata* means *three banded*.

S. trifasciata laurentii is an elegant plant, similar to the previous one. The dark-green markings are enclosed on the edges with bands in yellow color. It is called "goldband *Sansevieria.*" Although coming from the Congo, it is similar in growth and habits to the previous one.

S. trifasciata Hahnii is a sport (mutation) of the previous plant. In its transition it lost not only the golden bands but also the form. It does not have still, erect leaves, but forms a low rosette, maximum 12 inches across. The zigzag marking in dark green is less pronounced. Propagates from suckers grown at the base.

The ways of nature are amazing. The *S.t. Hahnii* lost golden bands as it developed from *S. t. laurentii*. However, another mutation of *S. Hahnii* surfaced with a broad, yellow band on wide leaves forming a low rosette. This is *S. trifasciata 'Golden Hahnii'*; it propagates from suckers that can be cut off and planted directly in a pot.

In watering *Sansevierias* it is important not to get water into the crown, which can result in rot. When overwatered, soft stem rot will attack the plant: it will become mushy at the base. *Sansevierias* are insect free.

Syngonium

Adapting from the humid rainforests of Central America to the dry atmosphere of our houses must have been quite a change for these plants. They demand very little: some filtered light and moist soil. They are even satisfied when the soil is dry. And on the contrary they will grow well in water only. The leaves are often narrow shaped, sometimes cleffed, and some varieties have leaves divided into three and more segments.

The chief attraction of *Syngoniums* is cream veining and blotching. In *S. auritum 'Fantasy'* half of the leaf is changed into silver and cream. The *S. albolineatum* has so much silver and white that the green color is edged out to outer fringes and some green blotches. *S. erythrophyllum* adds a reddish underside to its pink dots on green leaves. (The name *auritum* means *eared,* in reference to the two small leaves sticking like ears at the base of the leaf; *albolineatum* means *white-lined; erythrophyllum* means *red leaved.)*

Older *Syngoniums* spread with long shoots that can be cut and rooted in water or sandy peat to have new plants before the old ones become too straggly. The old name was *Nephthytis*.

Tradescantia
Wandering Jew

Somehow this trailing plant is always in the way. Any moist surface is a good spot to grow roots, which give it more vigor to reach even farther from its own pot to the neighboring pot, to the ground bed, to water in the pool — even carpet dampened by spilled water makes good ground for the roots. How can you lose with such a prolific grower, causing you only one worry: to keep it in its bounds?

The stems and leaves are succulent and small white flowers last one day, only to be supplemented by new flowers the next. Some named varieties have leaves striped with white and yellow and have a purple underside. Propagation is very easy, cuttings rooting in any medium. *Tradescantia* is named for John Tradescant, who explored in the seventeenth century for new plants in the Eastern portions of today's United States.

Vriesea

Vrieseas are some of the few *Bromeliads* not requiring much light. However, they want humid-

Zebrina pendula 'Quadricolor.'

ity, moist soil, and water in the center cup. These plants are not easy to propagate since they do not grow side shoots, only one in the center, which can be cut off and planted. That, of course, replaces only the original plant. The only means of multiplying is by seeds. It is named for a Dutch botanist, Dr. W. de Vriese.

V. hieroglyphica is called ''king of the *Bromeliads*'' for its large, dark-green and purple markings on light-green leaves, resembling Egyptian hieroglyphics. The bright-yellow flowers are carried on tall spikes.

The tall and narrow flowering spike gave the common name of ''flaming sword'' to *V. splendens*. The spike is orange or bright red, depending on the variety. Green leaves are marked with maroon bands. *Splendens* means *splendid*.

Zebrina Pendula

Quite often I am slow to appreciate the beauty of *Zebrinas*. Because they are lowly, undemanding plants, not requiring any attention, their beauty escapes my eyes. Only when grown in a prominent location, in a hanging basket or on a shelf, is their attractiveness displayed to the best advantage. The glistening silvery stripes on various shades of green or violet and vivid purple underside makes them lovely plants.

Closely related to *Tradescantias, Zebrinas* behave in the same way: they grow in any moist medium, spread rapidly wherever touching. Even the common name ''wandering Jew'' is applied to *Zebrinas* indiscriminately, just as it is to the *Tradescantias*.

The best colors belong to *Z. Quadricolor* (means *four color*) gaily banded cream, pink, silver, and purple. Such a coloring is, however, maintained in good light only. Also for propagation have to be selected only the cuttings in best coloring, to perpetuate nicely colored plants. Like most multicolored plants, this one also requires higher humidity and no cold drafts. *Zebrinas* are from Mexico. *Pendula* means *hanging*.

25
Foliage Plants

Next to a group of blooming or colorful plants, the ones having a plain green mantel look like Cinderellas. Yet as plain, simple workers, the foliage plants perform on places where their richer cousins would not survive. Colorful and blooming plants need sufficient light, humidity, and moisture to maintain their beauty.

The strength and acceptance of "Cinderellas" is in their ability to adapt to very difficult conditions of the captivity of our homes. Is there not enough light? Is the air dry and watering often omitted? Turn to the foliage plants. They are an indispensable part of ornaments in our homes.

Foliage Plants For Structures with Light-transmitting Roof

Aloysia Triphylla
Lemon Verbena

The old name for this plant was Lippia citriodora, sometimes also called *citronalis*. As the name indicates it is an herb of lemon fragrance. The yellowish-green, narrow leaves about 3 inches long are used to give lemon flavor to tea, drinks, jellies, etc. Even dry leaves keep the aroma for a long time. Flowers are not significant, being very small, on long spikes. It needs good light, even sun, and moderately moist soil. Propagation is from cuttings rooted in sand. An insect-free, undemanding plant, it comes from Chile and Argentina. *Triphylla* means *three leaved*.

Begonias

B. convolvulacea is one of few trailing *Begonias*. The palegreen leaves grow on long shoots that can be trained on a trellis or let hang gracefully down. The clusters of white flowers in winter will also pollinate itself, because the pollen from male flowers is shed on lower clusters of female flowers. It can stand heavy watering or dry soil and needs shade. Cuttings root in moist sand. Comes from Brazil. The name means *like a twine*.

B. epipsila is from Brazil, and is a low, spreading plant with thick, shiny, deep-green leaves and equally shiny and red underside. It has white flowers in winter. It requires moist soil, shade, and humidity, propagates from cuttings rooted in sand. The name means *bare above*, for the fact that hair covers all parts of the plant except the top of the leaves.

B. kenworthyi is named for a *Begonia* grower. The large, starlike leaves of dark green have pale midrib and underside pinkish. The rhizome looks like a thick stem. It wants good light and moderately dry soil. It has white flowers in winter and propagates from rhizome cuttings. Comes from Mexico.

B. leptotricha is called "woolly bear" for its brown, fuzzy underside of leaves. The dark-green, shiny leaves are cupped. It blooms in summer for a long time with white flowers, and requires bright light and very, very dry soil. Watering once a week in hot summer and once in two to three weeks in winter is sufficient. It is a fairly small and durable *Begonia* from Paraguay. The name means *thin hair*. Propagates from cuttings in sand, which has to be barely moist, and better from seeds.

B. paulensis looks like a light-green spiderweb on a green background. A rhizomatous *Begonia* from Brazil with almost round leaves, it needs shade and moderately dry soil. Flowers are cream colored with red bristles. Named for grower Pauli from Sao Paulo, Brazil.

B. purpurea looks more like a palm. The red, tall stalks carry a number of leaflets forming palmlike leaves. This unusual form makes it more attractive than its greenish flowers appearing in winter. Comes from Brazil and needs shade amd moist soil. Rhizomatous and propagates from sections of rhizome or seeds. *Purpurea* means *purple*, which does not apply to this plant.

Bischofia Javanica
Toog tree

A decorative container tree for a well-lit room. The leaves are finely toothed and grow in groups of three. Flowers are insignificant, small and greenish. Female flowers bear small reddish or bluish fruit. An insect-free plant, it should be kept moderately dry. As the name indicates, *Bischofia* comes from Java.

Carica Papaya
Papaya; Melon Tree

The well-known tropical fruit tree can be also grown in an indoor garden. However, the melon-like fruit cannot be readily expected. First, papaya has flowers of different sexes on different trees. Secondly, it needs full sun. The first problem can be circumvented by purchasing a variety having grafted branches of both sexes on one trunk and then pollinate manually. The demand for full sun can be fulfilled by planting papaya in a container that is moved outside for summer. In winter one can enjoy the deeply lobed, large leaves. Propagation is by seeds. An insect-free plant it should be kept moderately moist. Its origin is Colombia, and it is now grown for its fruit in all tropical countries. The name *Carica* is of mixed origin.

Cryptomeria Japonica Nana
Dwarf Japanese Cedar

An evergreen tree with one-inch needles curved inward. In mild climates of China and Japan, its native land, it is used extensively in gardens. It grows well in a container. Not only an ornamental tree, it is also insect free. Needs good light, even sun and moist soil.

Costus
Ginger

The aromatic ginger family needs generally good light, warmth, and high humidity to grow well and to flower. Fortunately, few of the gingers are more adapted to the conditions of an indoor garden, where light is filtered and humidity not so high. These Costus need moderately moist soil.

C. malortieanus from Costa Rica, is called "spiral ginger." The thick stalks carry long leaves in bright green with darker stripes, covered with shining hair. Grows to 3 feet in height. Flowers are yellow.

C. speciosus is from India. Its common name is "stepladder plant," in allusion to the leaves arranged in spiral around the stalk like steps. Leaves are smaller, shiny and pointed. Flowers are yellow. *Speciosus* means *showy*.

Propagation is by division of rootstock in spring. A better way is to root sections of stem 1 to 2 inches long, slightly covered with peatmoss under cover with the help of bottom heat.

Leucothoe Catesbaei
Sweet Bells

This evergreen shrub from the eastern United States is native to Virginia and Georgia. The glossy leaves form a nice background for clusters of white flowers bursting forth in May. As a member of the heath family, it needs rich soil with large amounts of acid peat moss. Soil should be kept acid and moist. An insect-free plant, it propagates from cuttings or seeds. Named for the daughter of a mythological king of Babylonia.

Foliage Plants for Solid-roof Structures

Aglaonema
Chinese Evergreen

Most *Aglaonemas* have variegated foliage. The well-known and grown house plant *Aglaonema modestum (sinensis),* called "Chinese evergreen," has long leaves, ribbed and plain green. A very durable plant, modest in its requirements, it will grow in almost any location. It blooms as a small plant with white spadix enclosed in a green spathe. It takes dry soil conditions, and will also grow in water. Propagation is from cuttings rooted in sand or water, as well as by division of old plants. *Modestum* means *modest.*

Araucaria Excelsa
Norfolk Island Pine

Discovered by Captain Cook on a small Norfolk Island, east of Australia, where it grows to height of 200 feet and covers the island instead of palms. In its juvenile form it refreshes any room with its beautiful proportions and greenery. The rate of growth depends on moisture, fertilizer, and humidity. If kept dry and if fertilizer is given only once or twice a year, it will grow two to three inches yearly. Plenty of moisture, fertilizing every two months, and humid atmosphere will result in growth of 12 to 18 inches per year. The one in our garden room grew 50 inches in three and a half years; that represents an annual growth of 14 inches. Similar *Araucaria* I observed in an office grew barely 3 inches in one year, due to the low humidity, lack of watering and fertilizing, and despite good light next to the large window.

Propagation is by seeds. It can be also done by rooting the terminal cutting in sand; however, the original tree will be disfigured. Such a propagation is in place when this beautiful tree outgrows its headroom. It is an excellent house plant. *Excelsa* means *tall.*

Aspidistra Elatior
Parlor Palm

This plant can stand so much abuse and bad growing conditions that it is called "cast-iron plant." Almost insect free, it will grow in any corner, even in a cold location. The green leaves, up to two feet long, grow on tall stalks. The decorative form *Variegata* has broad, white stripes, which will disappear if the plant is heavily fertilized or grown in rich, humusy soil. *Aspidistra* can take very low light levels. In fact, strong light can cause yellowing of leaves. Overwatering will cause root rot. Propagation is by division of root stock. It comes from China. *Elatior* means *taller.*

Ananas Comosus
Pineapple

One of the most delicious fruits we know is the pineapple, an outstanding member of the *Bromeliad* family. It was cultivated for its fruit in Brazil long before the discovery of America. A plant can be obtained easily from fresh pineapple fruit, always sold with a green crown of leaves. After cutting away the crown, all fleshy parts of fruit should be scraped away up to hard base and let to dry for one or two days. Then the green crown is set on moist sand to root. (I have seen it root in water also, but it takes much longer.) Transplanted into soil, it will grow into a nice plant with arching leaves covered with small spines. *Ananas* is a modified form of the name used by Amazon river Indians for pineapple. *Comosus* means *with long hair.*

A. comosus nanus is a dwarf pineapple often sold by florists with miniature fruit rising high above the plant. *Nanus* means *dwarf.*

Several varieties of variegated pineapple are on the market. All have leaves striped with ivory bands of different widths, some have red spines and rose tinted centers. However, they are quite expensive plants.

All pineapples can be propagated from offshoots growing from the base of the plant or even by stem suckers appearing below the fruits.

Begonias

B. erythrophylla 'Bunchii' is called "lettuce leaf *Begonia.*" The light-green leaves have ruffled edges tinted pink. Older leaves turn pink and almost white, providing a nice combination of colors. It has pink flowers in winter. Needs some shade and dry soil. It is rhizomatous.

B. erythrophylla feastii is the well-known "beefsteak *Begonia*," so called for its red underside of rounded leaves having high green gloss. It has pink flowers in winter. Wants shade and moist soil. It has been long cultivated as a house plant, and is rhizomatous. The name *erythrophylla* means *red leaved.*

B. ricinifolia is another *Begonia* grown for a long time as a houseplant, having one of the largest leaves among *Begonias*. The fresh green leaves are deeply cut and similar to the leaves of the *Ricinus,* the castor bean; hence the name. The leaves have a taffeta sheen and are covered with bristles. Large panicles of small, pink flowers are carried on stalks up to three feet tall (on older plants). Rhizomatous, blooming in winter, it propagates easily from rhizome cuttings and also from leaf. It needs shade and is not particular about moisture.

Brassaia Actinophylla (Schefflera)
Australian Umbrella Tree

One of the best indoor foliage plants. In its native Australia grows into a large tree. An admirable and durable house plant, it will take full sun, tolerate poor light, and does not want to be pampered. Needs dry soil. If too wet or if water stands in the bottom of the pot, leaf drop occurs. The large leaves are divided into segments—when young only three, in older plants up to sixteen segments. Regardless of the size, this plant provides a cheerful atmosphere wherever grown. Propagation is by seeds or by air layering. The name *Schefflera* is used in honor of a German citizen.

Cissus Rhombifolia
Grape Ivy

A grateful climber, Cissus grows and prospers without much attention and will survive without much watering. If kept moist, it grows fast. The rhombic, dark-green leaves gave it its name. Although a close relative of *Cissus discolor,* this vine is from the West Indies and South America. A good house plant, cuttings root easily in moist sand. *Cissus* is Greek for *ivy*.

Colocasia
Elephant Ear

The common name indicates large leaves. And they are, growing easily 2 to 3 feet in length on tall stalks. Colocasia needs high humidity, warmth and large amounts of water. *Colocasias* grow from tubers that are edible after boiling and are the staple food (taro) on many tropical islands. The flower is typical of the *Arum* family; thick spadix enclosed by a spathe in different colors (similar to the blossom of *Philodendron*). It is an insect-free plant.

C. antiquorum fontanesii has green leaves edged in purple; stems are brown. It is from Ceylon. *Antiquorum* means *of the ancients*.

C. antiquorum illustris is very attractive. The leaf is brown in purple shade, intersected by veins in light-green areas. Stems are green, sometimes violet. It comes from the East Indies. *Illustris* means *brilliant*.

C. esculenta is at home on Hawaii and other tropical islands. The fresh green leaves are quilted. *Esculenta* means *edible*.

Cordyline Terminalis
Hawaiian "Ti" Plant

Often sold as small logs in stores or brought as a souvenir from Hawaii, *cordyline* is a utility plant of its native lands: the Polynesian islands. Its leaves were used for roof covering of huts and for hula skirts; it also played a prominent part in religious ceremonies.

The leaves always form a terminal rosette of graceful curves; the lower leaves fall off as the plant inches up in height. If too tall and unsightly looking, the top can be cut off and put in a vase as an indoor decoration. Water should be changed occasionally. After several weeks roots will sprout. The stem can be cut into sections, which will be starters of new plants. Each section should have several eyes; the logs are half buried in soil, which should be kept moist. If a short stump is left on the mother plant and the soil is kept a little moist, it will also sprout.

Several varieties of the "Ti" plant are available. The common, greenleaved variety is a good house plant. The more colorful *Cordyline* hybrids have foliage colored in red and copper. The variety

'Tricolor' has leaves striped in pink, red, and cream on a green background. However, these beauties require more light, even mild sun, to keep their coloring. Warmth, humidity, and moist soil are their preference. The name *Cordyline* means *club,* in reference to the thick roots.

Crassula

Although they come from South Africa and love sun, these plants easily adapt to house conditions. Their leaves are generally thick, and fleshy, indicating the need for little watering; once a week is sufficient for good growth. They are slow growing, and for that property they are used in dish gardens, even if many of them will eventually grow into large proportions. Propagation is very easy from cuttings in sand and even better from leaves, which form roots and plantlets if laid on moist sand.

C. arborescens (silver dollar) is a heavy-set plant. The thick leaves are silver-gray with reddish edges. It is a nice pot plant. *Arborescens* means *like a tree*. (It grows in the wild 10 feet tall.)

C. argentea is known as "jade plant." It forms a very thick stem and branches carrying thick, shiny, jade-green leaves. It grows like a tree and is as heavy as lead. *Argentea* means *silvery,* a name that does not apply here.

C. 'Tricolor jade' is a hybrid. The leaves are pointed and variegated in gray, white, and pink—a very nice plant.

Crassula means *thick*. Avoid spraying with Malathion.

Ferns

An instant exotic atmosphere is created with ferns. The more so because in northern climates the fern is almost unknown, even if quite a few are native. Ferns seek the shade of large trees, and the darkness and dampness of the inner forest. The gracefully curved fronds of lacy foliage bring a different feeling to a room.

The affinity for shade and dampness is present in tropical ferns also. Many are difficult to maintain indoors, but a small number will make good house plants. That goes especially for *Pteris* ferns, which not only can stand neglect, but also offer variegated foliage, so uncommon among the ferns.

Adiantum raddianum (also known as *cuneatum*) is the well-known "Maidenhair fern." Coming from Brazil, it has been cultivated for a long time and used as a house plant. It needs shade and constantly moist soil. *Raddianum* means *radiating*. *Cuneatum* means *wedge shaped.*

Adiantum tenerum 'Wrightii' is called "fan maidenhair" for its large leaflets. Grows smaller than *raddianum* plant. From tropical South America, it must have shade and moist soil all the time. The word *tenerum* means *tender*. Both can be propagated by division of rootstock.

Asplenium bulbiferum has a name describing the feature of this fern: bulb bearing. Often called "hen and chicken fern," it forms small bulbils on the upper part of its fronds. The fronds can be bent and fastened to the top of a pot with moist peat moss to allow bulbils to root.

Asplenium nidus does not even look like a fern, with its wide blades. The common name "bird nest fern" describes both the nest-forming crown and its Latin name. It is good looking but has to be kept moist.

One of the best ferns for indoor culture is *Cibotium schiedei,* called "Mexican tree fern." It is very often used in decorating for its gracefully spreading form and beautiful green color, and also because it is not fussy. It can stand ocasionally dry soil. Propagation is from spores only.

Cyrtomium ferns are very good house plants, taking abuse and requiring minimum care. *Cyrtomium falcatum,* called also "fishtail fern," grows only two feet high. *Falcatum* means *sickle shaped. Cyrtomium falcatum 'rochefordianum,'* called "holly fern," has shiny leaves toothed on the edge. It is a small plant, about twelve inches high. *Cyrtomiums* grow well in regular potting soil with some peat moss added. Both plants like a cooler location.

The "Boston fern" - *Nephrolepis exaltata bostoniensis* — has nothing else in common with the city of Boston, except that it was discovered there as a chance variety in a shipment of ferns from Florida in 1894. Whereas the parent fern has more upright habit and is called "sword fern," the Boston fern bends gracefully. It is a good house plant but does not like cold drafts. It is propagated from runners found on the mother plant.

Strange looking ferns are "staghorn ferns" — *Platyceriums*. Of epiphytic nature, they are grown wired to a piece of wood or in a basket of peat moss, which has to be kept moist. Requiring shade and high humidity, they are not so well suited for a garden room.

Several ferns are unusually painted cream and white. These belong to the group of *Pteris,* consisting of mostly small plants often called "table ferns." Three cultivars have variegations on their fronds: *Pteris cretica 'Albo-lineata'* has, according to its name *'Albo-lineata,'* white lines in the center of the leaves. It grows only twelve inches. high. *Cretica* means *from Crete. Pteris ensiformis 'Victoriae'* called "silver table fern," grows to fourteen inches in height and has a creamy feather design in the center of its fronds. *Ensiformis* means sword shaped. An unusual name has *Pteris quadriaurita 'Agryaea,'* which means: *four-eared silver Pteris,* in allusion to the four small leaflets sitting below the main one. However, all leaflets have a wide, silvery band running through the center. It grows to the height of three feet. Another tall grower is *Pteris tremula* — "trembling fern" — which is not variegated but has nice fronds. *Pteris* ferns are the best ones for keeping and do very well as house plants. Not fussy about soil and watering, they can stand dry conditions, and require only what a regular room gives them: shade and warmth. The name *Pteris* means *wing.* Avoid spraying *Pteris* fern with Malathion.

Ficus elastica 'Variegata.'

Ficus
Rubber Plant

The edible fig, which gave the name to the whole family, does not look like the ornamental foliage plant so common in cultivation. The milky juice of *Ficus elastica,* yielding elastic latex is still the source of rubber in India.

Ficus elastica grown in a pot is an almost indispensable house plant. It is loved for its thick, shiny, and stout leaves. A variety *Variegata* has leaves variegated in gray and cream. Much better is *F. elastica Doescheri,* developed in New Orleans. The leaves are blotched in gray, white, and cream; midrib and stalks are pink.

F. lyrata (pandurata) has large thick leaves in the form of a violin — hence, the common name: fiddle-leaf fig. It is a good decorator.

F. retusa nitida is often seen as large trees decorating commercial offices. *Retusa* means *notched; nitida* means *shining*.

F. stricta or *philippinense* has shining leaves on arching branches. It is easily recognized by water pores scattered along the edges. Used as a large, decorative tree with gracefully bending branches, and called "weeping fig." *Stricta* means *upright*.

"Rubber plant" has great latitude in light requirements: from full sun to very poor light. Soil should be kept moderately dry, although I have had a *Ficus stricta* on wick watering for three years and it is growing well. *Ficus* plants like warmth and resent cold drafts. If located near outside door, the frequent opening of the door in winter will kill any rubber plant. Propagation is by air layering (mossing).

Geranium – Pelargonium

Pelargoniums, or by common name *geraniums* are not suitable for a garden room full of tropical plants — that is, if you expect them to bloom. *Pelargoniums* set their buds at quite low night temperatures of 45°-55°F. If the temperature is kept above 55°F at night, *Geraniums* will not bloom; they will just grow into nice foliage plants.

It is always possible to bring into flowering a few *pelargoniums* if they are put into the coldest corner where the light is bright and sun can reach. Even building some shelves in such a corner is advantageous in inducing them to bloom.

Not all *Pelargoniums* are grown for flowers. *Geraniums* copy the fragrance of some other plants. Their leaves, when touched or rubbed, give off the smell of rose, apple, lemon, peppermint, nutmeg, or pine. *Pelargonium capitatum* and *P. graveolens* are rose scented and are used for the production of the precious rose oil in perfumes. The lemon fragrance is locked in leaves of *P. crispum. P. odoratissimum* has the scent of apple, and *P. fragrans* is nutmeg scented. *P. tomentosum* has very beautiful leaves, smaragd green and velvety, and has the fragrance of peppermint. Many scented *geraniums* have leaves so different from the well-known garden types that they would not be recognized as *Geraniums*. The most remote form has *P. filicifolium* (the name describes the leaf: *fern leaved),* which has a pungent scent. Similar to it is *P. denticulatum* with slightly toothed leaves, just as its name says. This one is pine scented.

All the fragrant *Geraniums* grow well in the garden room or in the house. They do not bloom there and are satisfied with filtered light, in direct contrast to another group of fancy leaved *Geraniums,* which need bright light and sun to maintain the brilliantly colored leaves. Quite a number of fancy-leaved *Geraniums* are available. Perhaps the best known are: *Pelargonium hortorum 'Skies of Italy'; P. hortorum 'Miss Burdett-Coutts';* and *P. hortorum. 'Mrs. Cox.'*

Pelargoniums are native to the dry and mountainous areas of South Africa, where the night temperature is quite low, days hot and sunny without much rain. *Geraniums* want to have those conditions duplicated; however, they will be satisfied with less light if the soil is kept dry. Propagation is from cuttings in moist sand or even in regular potting soil.

The difference between the *Geranium* and *Pelargonium* is only in the technical character of the flower. The blossoms of *Pelargoniums* have two of the five petals slightly larger; also *Pelargoniums* have seven stamens but *Geraniums* have ten stamens. All our garden *Geraniums* and those mentioned above are *Pelargoniums*. True *Geraniums* are mostly wild flowers, some native to the United States.

The name *Geranium* means *crane*, for the seed pod resembling a crane's beak. *Pelargonium* in Greek means *stork*, for the similarity of the seed pod to a stork's beak.

Nicodemia Diversifolia
Indoor Oak

The leaves are shaped like oak leaves, but this plant does not belong to the oak family. It is grown for its leaves which have a blue metallic sheen. For this feature it was named *diversifolia: variable leaved*. From Madagascar, it wants moist soil, filtered light, and the warmth of a house or garden room. Propagation is from cuttings rooted in sand.

Osmanthus Fragans
Sweet Olive

Not a true olive although from the olive family, osmanthus can adapt very well to indoor growing conditons. The leaves are similar to those of holly, shiny and olive green. The white flowers are small, in clusters, but very fragrant and in bloom all winter and spring making the Sweet olive an appreciated house plant. Good light and moist soil are a necessity. Its home is the temperate zone of China and Japan. Cuttings of half-ripened wood, taken in summer, root in sand under cover. It is a very slow-growing plant. *Osmanthus* means *fragrant flower*.

Palms

The sign of tropics is the palm. Its slender trunk and graceful head definitely announce the warm climate. In cold areas it can be enjoyed only indoors, and then as a small specimen, not having the true palm character. But even as young plants, many palms are very graceful. And since the attraction is coupled with durability, they make good decorators. Just about any palm can be raised in a conservatory; the selection is quite restricted for a room with a solid roof.

Indoor palms need filtered light and an abundance of moisture. Watering is needed about every other day. The regular potting mixture can be made more water absorbent by addition of peat moss. Transplanting should be done only when really necessary, since palms do not mind being pot bound. Propagation is by seeds, with some palms by suckers.

Caryota mitis, called "dwarf fishtail palm," is an exotic-looking plant, with wide leaf segments ragged at the tips. Sprouting from the base with many stalks, it forms quite a dense plant. It needs a little more light and humidity than other palms suitable for indoor culture. Propagation is from suckers. *Mitis* means *gentle*.

Chamaedorea elegans is an elegant palm, growing well in dark places and in dry air. It grows fairly slowly. It is often listed as *Neanthe bella*.

Chamaedorea erumpens, or bamboo palm, has clusters of thin, tall stems like a bamboo. The young suckering reeds can be separated and potted. *Erumpens* means *emitting* (number of stems).

Howeia forsteriana, also known as "Kentia palm," growing on a little Lord Howe island between Australia and New Zealand, and is an important source of income for the inhabitants of that island. After flowering, the seeds form on the palms for six years, then are collected as a community project. The prime reason for which this palm is liked is the fullness of its leaves from bottom to top. The gracefully bent branches gave it the common name *paradise palm*.

Phoenix roebelenii is a dwarf belonging to the date palm group. Perhaps most known and cultivated of all indoor palms, its gracefully arching branches and durability made it so popular. *Phoenix* is the Greek name for *date*.

Rhapis excelsa, called "lady palm," grows slowly in many stems. The leaves are divided into 3 to 10 wide segments. It is best propagated by the division of suckers. This palm has to be kept on the dry side. The variegated form has ivory-striped leaf segments. *Excelsa* means *tall*.

Philodendron

For the introduction to the *Philodendron* see page 122. Most of the *Philodendron* belonging to this group can be bought from florists, being well-known and much-grown plants.

P. cruentum is called "red leaf *Philodendron,*" for its red underside of leaves, which make a nice contrast to the shiny green of the top of the leaves. *Cruentum* means *bloody*.

P. mandaianum puts the red of its stems and tips

Philodendron oxycardium.

of the leaves into contrast with dark green leaves.

P. oxycardium (also called *cordatum)* is very often sold as a climbing type. The heart-shaped leaves are dark green; the variety *"Variegatum"* has cream blotches. The name means *heart shaped.*

P. panduraeforme has differently shaped leaves: like a fiddle, hence, the name, which means *fiddle shaped.* Thick leaves are dark green.

Very well known is the "split leaf *Philodendron,*" *P. pertusum* (botanically *Monstera deliciosa).* The leaves are cut across the edges, which is an unusual occurence not found in many plants. If grown in insufficient light and humidity the leaves are smaller and the splitting is limited. A variety 'Variegatum' is also available, having large, yellow areas. The fruit is very tasty, therefore the name: *deliciosa,* meaning delicious; it tastes partly like banana and partly like pineapple, and it ripens in tropical areas.

P. selloum is a self-heading type with large, deeply cut and frilled leaves. It needs more space, as the long stalks, carrying large leaves spread considerably. It is an excellent decorator.

Propagation of *Philodendron* is by cuttings rooted in sand, even in water, or by air layering. Yellowing or browning of leaves is due to insufficient light. At times the cause can also be a lack of fertilizer and a pot bound plant.

Pleomele

Sometimes called *Dracaena,* to which it is related, *Pleomele* is a good house plant. Its leaves are similar to the *Dracaena* or to Hawaiian 'Ti' plant. Filtered light and moist soil are to their liking. Propagation is by sections of stem with several "eyes," half buried lengthwise, in sand or soil.

P. reflexa has short and narrow leaves thickly crowded and bent back on the self-heading stem. *Reflexa* means *bent back.*

The variegated form is called "Song of India." Two wide, yellow bands along the edges with green center having two narrow stripes make it a very nice plant. Slow growing, it requires warmth and humidity. It is not suitable for house culture.

Podocarpus Macrophylla

Southern Yew

Also called "Japanese yew" for the similarity of the narrow leaves. This very ornamental plant of bushy growth is planted often in the South. Its pleasant green, very narrow, needlelike leaves are several inches long and in nice contrast to the light-green branches. Although slow growing, it eventually reaches large proportions when grown outdoors. But it can be easily sheared to the desired shape and still retain its beauty. It is a very good house plant, needing filtered light and moist soil. It prefers a cool location. Propagation is by cutting in sand with the help of bottom heat. The name *Podocarpus* is made from words meaning *foot* and *fruit. Macrophyllus* means *having long leaves.*

Scindapsus

Scindapsus is a well-known and cultivated house plant, also called *"Pothos."* The heart-shaped leaves are generally variegated with blotches in different colors. *S. aureus* (means *golden*) has yellow spots, and its variety *'Marble Queen'* almost white blotches. *S. pictus* and *S. pictus argyreus* have leaves marked with silver spots (*pictus* means *painted; argyreus: silvery).* These two like the soil to be more moist; the first two plants require quite dry soil.

Scindapsus are climbers attaching themselves to any support, like English ivy. They can also be grown on a table and the long runners laid freely in a circle around the pot. Coming from Borneo and the Solomon islands, they can take high temperatures but dislike cold drafts. Will also live happily in dark corners; however, when grown in good light, the markings on the leaves are much larger and of better colors. Cuttings root easily in moist sand. It is an insect-free plant.

Senecio Mikanioides

Parlor Ivy; German Ivy

Fresh green and soft leaves resembling ivy are characteristic of this plant. Used for a long time as a house plant, it thrives in bright light either hanging down or climbing on some support. In poor light its leaves stay small and are without luster. Besides good light it needs moist soil.

Planted in a ground bed, parlor ivy spreads quickly and soon forms a dense ground cover. As it creeps along, it roots almost at every node, densely covering the ground bed. However, it will choke any soft-stem plant it encounters, especially *Coleus* and *Impatiens*. The dense covering causes stem rot on other plants, which die. Older plants bloom with small, yellow, fragrant flowers. It does not have much in common with Germany, since it comes from South Africa. Cuttings root very easily in moist sand. *Mikanioides* means *resembling mikania*.

26
What Is Missing?

Many well-known, even desirable, plants are not listed in the preceding catalogue. For many there is a reason for such an omission.

The plants just listed are tropicals requiring shade of some degree. The shade necessary for plants and people alike makes it impossible to bring into bloom the sun-loving *Geraniums* and *Cacti*. The *Cacti* have another limitation: even in large numbers they do not provide the gardenlike atmosphere for which we strive.

From the tropicals were omitted Bird of Paradise (*Strelitzia reginae)* and Kafir lily (*Clivia miniata*). Although beautiful plants, especially in bloom, it takes seven years before they flower for the first time. That fact will disappoint some. Another plant bringing disappointment is *Gardenia*, whose beautiful, fragrant flowers can be enjoyed only where the exact temperature and humidity are maintained to prevent the drop of buds.

And of course *Orchids*. Claims were made that *Orchids* are easy to grow, which is the truth about many. However, *Orchids* have a number of special requirements starting with special growing medium (*osmunda* fiber or tree bark), notched pots, and ending with necessary low night temperature for forming of buds for many. The terrestrial *Orchids*, growing in regular soil, are not that numerous. *Orchids* are a fascinating hobby, as proven by 12,000 members of the American Orchid Society. However, most *Orchid* growers specialize in *Orchids* and grow few other plants besides.

A wealth of beautiful and large blossoms or colorful leaves can be obtained from plants growing from bulbs. Most of the bulbs require a rest period in a dark, cool place and again to bring them back into the indoor garden when they show signs of new growth. This extra effort was eliminated to make garden room duties more acceptable, the only exception being *Gloxinia*.

All this elimination of many beautiful, fragrant, and even easy-to-care for plants was done to make an indoor garden a more enjoyable room—a true room of delight.

27
Going Away on a Trip

Probably the most worrisome time for every owner of an indoor garden or home greenhouse is vacation time, more so if it is not easy to find someone to take care of the plants. It is possible to dispense with a caretaker, provided certain precautions are taken.

Twice I left our room of delight without anybody's care: once for four days, on another occasion for six days in hot summer, when outdoor temperatures were 85° - 95° F. It worked well. The key to such unguarded absence is: a number of bowls of sufficient size. Each plant in a pot is set into a bowl filled with water. The plant's water requirements and its size dictate the size of the bowl. The larger and thirstier the plant, the larger the bowl.

I have to hasten to say that many plants will get by for a week without being set into a bowl of water. To this category belong: *Aralias, Araucaria excelsa, Begonias* (only these: hairy leaf, *masoniana, rhizomatous, semperflorens), Bougainvilleas, Bromeliads, Cacti, Ceropegia woodii, Chlorophytum, Cissus rhombifolia, Cordyline terminalis, Crotons, Dieffenbachias, Dracaenas, Euonymus, Episcia dianthiflora, Euphorbias, Ficus, Geraniums, Hoya carnosa, Kalanchoes, Oxalis, Peperomias, Pileas, Pittosporum, Podocarpus, Rhoeo discolor, Sansevierias, Schlumbergera bridgessii, Scindapsus, Syngoniums, and Zygocactus truncatus.*

All these plants need only to be well watered before you leave and will do well for seven days in hot summer. Similar care is given to plants growing in ground beds. I water the beds well for two days before and again flood them just before leaving on a trip. In this manner no additional watering is needed for seven days.

The bulk of favorite plants needs more water and a provision for supplying it. For plants arranged for wick watering no change is necessary. The exception might be some needing large quantities of water — like *Strobilathes, Impatiens, Manettia, Medinilla, Dipladenia* — and would need to have their regular bowl exchanged for a larger one.

Many plants not grown on wick watering will tolerate for few weeks standing in a bowl of water. From my experiments with 125 plants on wick watering I learned that damage does not occur to the plants on wick watering before six weeks. (The first plants to suffer from too much water on wick watering were *Geraniums* which have to be kept dry, and *Begonia cathayana* known for its exact requirements.)

When plants were left with such precautions for four days no damage was found. On another trial of six days only three casualties were counted. One was *Begonia cathayana,* beautiful, but touchy. Had I left it only well watered it would have survived. But standing in a large plate of water was too much moisture for it. The two other casualties suffered from a lack of water; they should have been put in larger bowls of water. Pineapple sage dryed up; the *Fuchsia Gartenmeister Bohnstedt* lost quite a few leaves, kept on producing blossoms, but later succumbed. These were unexpected losses, due to the insufficient knowledge of exact requirements of plants involved in this experiment. Actually I was more worried about *Aeschynanthus lobbianus* growing in a large hanging basket, which was not arranged for wick watering. It received only good watering — and survived six days without loss of blossoms. These few examples show the varied tolerance of plants. Some have very narrow limits of endurance, others are flexible in their fight for survival.

It is advantageous to take some plants and put them into the house proper. *Anthurium andraeanum and Begonias (cathayana* and *rex)* will do better in the house.

To put a large amount of plants into bowls might seem like too much work. It depends on the plants grown in a indoor garden. I have during summer about 320 plants. At the time of the six-day experiment without caretaker, 38 plants were on wick watering and another seven had wick in the pot. In addition to this I put 114 plants into the bowls. Most of them were molded from Plexiglas. The great majority were of one-quart capacity, others holding almost half a gallon of water. About 30 were regular cereal or soup bowls, useful for small plants. A number of ''bowls'' were nothing more than large aluminum pie pans.

Such an arrangement for vacation trips is not limited to six days only. It is easier to find somebody who will come once a week, water all plants, and fill bowls with water — without fear of doing something improperly. What turns many people away from the care of plants is the uncertainty of proper care.

Epilogue

Flowers have their people, not to own but to captivate. People fascinated by flowers and plants perform acts some consider foolish, others unnecessary, still others silly. Whoever comes under the spell of flora is a happy person. Men and women enchanted by flowers are enriched, led to relaxation and appreciation of beauty. The flowery obsession is harmless yet rewarding, laborious yet relaxing; humble as the soil the plants need but culminating in beauty no man can create. In nature flowers do not need people. Yet if men cooperate with plants the result is greater beauty and production of the flowery world.

Flowers have their people.

Appendix

List of House Plants

Aechmea: discolor
fulgens
Aglaonemas
Araucaria excelsa
Allophyton mexicanum
Ananas comosus
Ardisia crispa
Aspidistra elatior
Begonia: erythrophylla
rex 'King Edward IV'
ricinifolia
Bischofia javanica
Brassaia actinophylla (Schefflera)
Ceropegia woodii
Chlorophytums
Cissus rhombifolia
Clusias
Coffea arabica
Columnea 'Cornelian'
Cordyline terminalis
Crassulas
Cryptanthus
Dieffenbachias
Dracaenas
Ferns: Adiantum raddianum
(Maidenhair fern)
Cibotium schiedei
Cyrtomiums
Nephrolepis exaltata
(Boston fern)
Pteris (table ferns)
Ficus
Fittonias
Fuchsia "Gartenmeister Bohnstedt"
Geraniums (Scented Leaf)
Gynuras
Hoya carnosa
Iresine
Kalanchoe: pinnata
tomentosa
Marantas
Mimosa pudica
Neoregelias
Nicodemia diversifolia
Nidulariums
Osmanthus: fragrans
ilicifolius variegatus
Palms
Pandanus
Peperomias
Philodendrons
Pileas
Pittosporum
Plectranthus
Pleomele reflexa
Podocarpus
Rhoeo discolor
Rosa roulettii
Saintpaulia (Afrian violet)
Sansevierias
Scindapsus (Pothos)
Senecio micanioides
Syngoniums
Tradescantias
Vriesias
Zebrinas

Terrarium plants:

Begonia: crispula
imperialis smaragdina
rajah
versicolor
Selaginella krausiana
Sinningia: 'Doll Baby'
'Pink Flare'
pusilla

This list represents one hundred thirty eight house plants (not including the African violets) described in this book.

Sources of Plants

In recent years a larger selection of exotic plants

had become available from local florists and even department stores. Generally these outlets sell mostly dependable house plants. Lately however, many have introduced tropical plants that are less adaptable to house conditions, but that are sold for their attractive foliage to brighten the long winter months. I was very surpised when my wife discovered the beautiful *Maranta erythroneura* in a large discount store. I found this *Maranta* even in a dime store. It also surprised me to find, in a greenhouse of a florist, a nice selection of *rex Begonias*, some *Bromeliads*, and even such exotics, as *Strobilanthes dyerianyus*. In another greenhouse I found several *Episcias* among them the yellow-flowering 'Tropical Topaz.'

In buying of tropical plants, the best way is to visit the greenhouses, directly rather than the store, of the florist. In the greenhouse the selection of plants is larger and more varieties are available. The best time to buy plants from local greenhouse is from fall to spring, when florists sell only indoor plants.

Many exotics, however, have to be ordered from growers specializing in tropical plants, issuing catalogues and selling by mail. The shipments of tropical plants are limited to a few months of the year, generally from May to June and September to October. July and August are too hot for shipping of the plants. It normally takes three to six weeks from the time of ordering to the delivery of tropicals. If you order too late in the fall, it may happen that the delivery will be postponed until the next spring.

Mail order catalogs:

Indicated price for a catalog is generally deductable from the first order, depending on the grower.

Alberts & Merkel Bros. Inc., Boynton Beach, Florida, 33435.
Primarily *Orchids; Bromeliads*; Tropical plants. 50c;

Buell's Greenhouses, Eastford, Conn. 06242.
African violets and *Gesneriads* only. 25c;

Edelweiss Gardens, Robbinsville, N.J. 08691.
Begonias, Bromeliads, Tropical plants. 35c;

Fischer Greenhouses, Linwood, N.J. 08221.
African violets, *Gesneriads*. 15c;

International Growers Exchange Inc. P.O.Box 397, Farmington, Mich. 48024.
Tropical plants, *Orchids*. $2.00

Kartuz Greenhouses, Wilmington, Mass. 01887
Gesneriads, Begonias, Tropical plants, 35c;

Logee's Greenhouses, Danielson, Conn. 06239.
Begonias; Oxalis; Tropical plants. $1.00

McComb Greenhouses, New Straitsville, Ohio, 43766.
Tropical plants. 35c;

Park Seed Co. Greenwood, S.C. 29646.
Some tropical plants. Free

Roehr's Exotic Nurseries, Farmingdale, N.J. 07727.
Tropical plants. Free

Plant Societies

Some plant societies have permanent headquarters. Others are served by the members — officers from their own homes. This fact accounts for any change in address you might encounter when contacting them.

Plant societies are groups of people interested in particular plants, to stimulate and promote interest in those plants. To that goal each society has some publishing organ available to the members only. Many societies have a seed fund, selling seeds or plants to their members. Exchange of cuttings and plants among members is part of the activity.

Each society is composed of members at large and of those grouped into chapters, generally in large cities.

African Violet Society of America Inc.
P.O.Box 1326, Knoxville, Tenn. 37901.
African Violet Magazine, 5 times a year.

American Begonia Society Inc.
10331 S. Colima Road, Whittier, Cal. 90604
Monthly publication: *The Begonian.*

American Bromeliad Society
1811 Edgecliffe Dr. Los Angeles, Cal. 90026
Monthly bulletin.

American Gesneria society
Worldway Postal Center, Box 91192,
Los Angeles, Cal. 90009
Bi-monthly publication:
Gesneriad-Saintpaulia News

American Gloxinia and Gesneriad Society
P.O. Box 174, New Milford, Conn. 06776
Bi-monthly publication: *The Gloxinian.*

American Orchid Society, Inc.
Botanical Museum of Harvard University,
Cambridge, Mass. 02138
Monthly publication: *American Orchid Society Bulletin.*

International Fern Society
2433 Burritt Ave.
Redondo Beach, Cal. 90278
Monthly Newsletter.

Saintpaulia International
P.O. Box 10604, Knoxville, Tenn. 37919

Bi-monthly publication:
Gesneriad-Saintpaulia News.

Suppliers of Greenhouse Structures

Firms listed provide free catalogues on request, also a price list.

Aluminum Greenhouses, Inc.
14615 Lorain Avenue, Cleveland, Ohio, 44111

Ezyrected - Aluminum and Redwood greenhouses.
Texas Greenhouse Co. Inc. 2717 St. Louis Ave.
Fort Worth, Texas, 76110

Ickes - Braun Glasshouses.
P.O.Box 147, Deerfield, Ill. 60015

Lord and Burnham Inc.
Irvington, N.Y. 10533 or
Des Plaines, Ill. 60016

Redfern's Prefab Greenhouse Mfg. Co,
55 Mt. Hermon Road, Scotts Valley, Cal. 95060
(Redwood greenhouses with double glazing)

Skylight, Domes, Transport Walls and Roofs:

Suppliers listed offer catalogues, which are examples of possible combinations of their systems, applicable to desired needs.

EPI Architectural Systems,
1844 Ardmore Bldv., Pittsburgh, Pa. 15221
(skylights; transparent and translucent roofs)

Fisher Skylights Inc.
2856 Webster Ave., Bronx, N.Y. 10458

Hillsdale Industries Inc.
Hillsdale, Mich. 49242
(skylight and space enclosures)

Ickes - Braun Inc.
P.O.Box 147, Deerfield, Ill. 60015
(domes; skylights; enclosures)

Kalwall Corp.
88 Pine Street, Manchester, N.H. 03103
(translucent walls and roof systems; double glazing.)

Lord and Burham Inc.
Irvington, N.Y. 10533 or
Des Plaines, Ill. 60016
(domes; space enclosures)

Naturalite Inc.
3233 West Kingsley Road, Garland, Texas 75040
(skylights; roofs)

Structures Unlimited Inc.
37 Union Street, Manchester, N.H. 03103
(skylights; space enclosures)

Super Sky Products Inc.
Thiensville, Wisc. 53092
(skylights; roof enclosures)

Temcor Crystogon
2825 Toledo Street, Torrance, Cal. 90503
(domes; roofs; space enclosures)

Evaporative cooler:

Essick Manufacturing Co.
1950 Santa Fe Ave. Los Angeles, Cal. 90021
or 3215 Brown Street, Little Rock, Ark. 72204
or 850 Woodruff Lane, Elizabeth, N.J. 07201

Watering attachment:

Bete Fog Nozzle Inc.
309 Wells Street, Greenfield, Mass. 01301
(Called by company "Brush Sprayer," has 36 inch aluminum extension, capable of accepting spray disks for fine spray)

Smaller watering attachment with 14 inch extension (about the same price) available from:
The House Plant Corner,
P.O.Box 810, Oxford, Mass. 21654

Suppliers of Garden Statues

Austin, — Art for the home
815 Grundy Avenue, Holbrook, L.I. N.Y.

Kenneth Lynch & Sons, Garden Ornaments
Wilton, Conn. 06897
180-page catalog $2.50

Suppliers of Fountains

Kim Lighting (Fountains, pumps, garden lights)
P. O. Box 1275
16555 E. Gale Avenue,
City of Industry, Calif. 91747

Roman Fountains
P. O. Box 10190
Albuquerque, N. M. 87114

Bibliography

Brilmayer, Bernice. *All about Begonias.* New York: Doubleday. 1960.

Graf, A. B. *Exotic Plant Manual.* Contains 4,200 illustrations and description of several thousands plants. East Rutherford: Roehrs, 1970.

Graf, A. B. *Exotica.* 6th Edition. Contains 12,000 illustrations and description of 9,000 plants. East Rutherford: Roehrs, 1973.

Kiaer, E. *Indoor Plants.* New York: Crown Publishers, 1965.

Moore, Harold, E. Jr. *African violets, Gloxinias and Their Relatives.* New York: McMillan, 1957.

Padilla, V. (editor) *Bromeliads in Color and Their Culture.* Los Angeles: Bromeliad Society, 1966.

Pirone, Pascal, P. *Diseases and Pests of Ornamental Plants.* Fourth Edition. New York: Ronald Press, 1970.

Schulz, Peggie (editor). *Gesneriads and How To Grow Them.* Grandview, Mo: Diversity Books, 1967.

Smith, Lyman, B. *The Bromeliads.* South Brunswick: Barnes, 1969.

Controlling insects on flowers. Agriculture information Bulletin No. 237. Washington, D. C. U. S. Department of Agriculture, 1967.

Exotic Plants. A Golden Nature Guide. New York: Western Publishing, 1971.

Insect-Pest Management and Control. Volume 3 of: *Principles of plant and animal pest control.* Publication 1695. Washington, D. C. National Academy of Sciences, 1969.

Brooklyn Botanic Garden publishes handbooks on indoor and outdoor gardening. List available from: Brooklyn Botanic Garden, 1000 Washington Ave. Brooklyn, N.Y. 11225

Under Glass, The home greenhouse Gardener's Magazine Bi-monthly by Burnham Corp. Irvington, N.Y. 10533

The listed books are only introductory. A large number of books is available, dealing with particular plants or plant families.

Index

Numbers in italics indicate photographs.